Stock Purchase Agreements Line by Line

A Detailed Look at Stock Purchase Agreements and How to Change Them to Meet Your Clients' Needs

Jaron R. Brown and Tyler E. Giles

ASPATORE

For additional copies or customer service inquiries, please e-mail west.customer.service@thomson.com.

ISBN 978-0-314-29221-6

Mat #41662341

ASPATORE

Aspatore Books, a Thomson Reuters business, exclusively publishes C-Level executives and partners from the world's most respected companies and law firms. Each publication provides professionals of all levels with proven business and legal intelligence from industry insiders—direct and unfiltered insight from those who know it best. Aspatore Books is committed to publishing an innovative line of business and legal titles that lay forth principles and offer insights that can have a direct financial impact on the reader's business objectives.

ACKNOWLEDGMENT

They say it takes a village to raise a child, an orchestra to play a symphony, and an army to win a war. While the authorship of this book was many orders of magnitude less complex than any of the foregoing, it could not have happened without the contributions of our friends, colleagues, family and editors. With that in mind, we would like to take a moment to recognize and thank the following individuals:

Special thanks to Shawn K. Baldwin for the guest note on negotiation strategies and tips found at the end of the introduction. Shawn is the Senior Vice President and Group Counsel at Equifax, Inc. (NYSE: EFX) where, among other things, he is in charge of Mergers & Acquisitions, Intellectual Property and Technology Transactions.

Many thanks to Joseph M. Costyn, who assisted us with the labor and employment sections of the book. Joey is a Georgia native with over ten years of legal study and practice in the fields of corporate litigation and employment law.

Many thanks to Robert W. Kamerschen for the guest note on the role of compliance in M&A transactions found in Section 4.12. Robbie is the SVP, General Counsel & Corporate Secretary of Aaron's Inc. (NYSE: AAN) and is, among other things, an expert in government compliance issues.

Many thanks to Ethan Thompson for the guest note on purchase price valuation included in Section 1.01. Ethan is currently a Director, New Initiatives, Product Management at McKesson Corporation (NYSE: MCK), and an expert in business valuation and strategic development.

Last (by virtue of alphabetical ordering), but certainly not least, many thanks to Leah L. Weinberg, who assisted us with the real estate sections of the book, including the guest note in Section 4.06. Leah is the Associate General Counsel at Rouse Properties, Inc. (NYSE: RSE) and is an expert in real estate law.

DEDICATION

We dedicate this book to our colleagues, friends and family. In the business of buying and selling significant assets, sometimes it is easy to forget that the most valuable assets are the relationships with those closest to you.

CONTENTS

Introduction

Buying and selling a business can be an extremely complex, time-consuming, and costly process. It typically involves two parties: a buyer and a seller. Each party customarily engages legal counsel, accountants, and other third-party advisors to guide it through the transaction process. If successful, the process typically results in the parties entering into a written definitive agreement to buy and sell the business, with the process ending once the transaction is consummated in accordance with the terms of the definitive agreement. In this book, we explore the provisions commonly found in a written definitive agreement for the purchase and sale of a business, which is accomplished by way of the transfer by one party to the other of 100 percent of the capital stock of the entity that operates the business.

What is the Purpose of a Definitive Agreement?

Generally

A businessperson who desires to execute a transaction will often remark to his or her lawyer: "we have a 'handshake-deal,' we've done business in the past, and we trust each other, so why do we need to spend a lot of time and money drafting agreements to reflect what we have already agreed to?" The answer—it is simply good business practice to set in writing an agreement to execute a business transaction, especially if the transaction is complex. It is good business practice for at least three reasons: (1) it facilitates deeper thought on, and thorough planning for, the contingencies and risk inherent in the transaction; (2) it sets forth a clear roadmap for the transaction, which can be used by the parties involved and uninvolved third parties who may have a need to know the details of the transaction; and (3) it often stops disputes between the parties before they arise, which can ultimately save the parties money at the end of the day.

Facilitation of Deeper Thought

Going through the process of putting an agreement to buy and sell a company into writing forces the parties to consider in detail all the contingencies and risk inherent in the transaction. The parties must come to terms with all the specific terms and conditions of the transaction, not simply the basic terms such as price and time of closing. Without a written agreement, parties may be more flippant in negotiating the details of the transaction, thinking that they can manage any issue that may arise if and when it does. Such an approach could subject the parties to unnecessary risk and ultimately lead to an inefficient or failed transaction. Creating a written agreement facilitates careful thought around the risks each party is willing to bear, confirms each party's due diligence with respect to the transaction and business, and potentially eliminates any possible gaps and uncertainty in the transaction. In the end, the process should help ensure that the outcome of the transaction was as agreed by the parties initially.

The Agreement as a Planning Tool

The process of buying and selling a business is often complex and can span over weeks and sometimes months. It usually requires the parties involved to take specific actions at certain times and upon the occurrence of certain events. With so many moving parts, it is highly unrealistic that the parties will be able to memorize every detail of the agreement they struck and the actions required to bring the transaction to a closing. A written agreement generally enables the parties to more effectively and efficiently perform the obligations to which they agreed because it sets forth in writing, as opposed to in the minds of the parties, the details of those obligations. In essence, a written agreement serves as a tangible roadmap and an illustration of the buy and sell agreement, memorializing the intent of the parties and outlasting parties' potentially fading memories. Additionally, a written agreement memorializing a transaction can be beneficial to individuals and other interested parties who were not part of the transaction negotiations, but who have a vested interest in the transaction. Buying and selling a company cannot be viewed as a transaction in a vacuum, as its effects often extend beyond the individuals who negotiated the transaction and the parties to the agreement. For example, if the buyer is seeking outside financing from a third party to buy the business, then that potential financing source will want to understand the terms and conditions of the transaction before committing to the financing.

Defusing Disputes

Because buying and selling a business is often a complex transaction that takes time to develop, as time passes, often the business's condition changes and the parties' expectations do so as well. Under such circumstances, without a written agreement, a party may either demand that the other party make concessions or attempt to avoid closing the transaction, which can often lead to disputes. Setting forth in a written agreement the details of how to deal with changed circumstances can help avoid such disputes. A written agreement governing the transaction can set forth clear obligations and rights with respect to changed circumstances. Once a party subjects itself to a written agreement, it is committing to such obligations and rights, which can be very costly to avoid. Without a written agreement, resolution of disputes hinges on the biased interpretation of the verbal agreement according to the parties' respective memories; therefore, a well-drafted written agreement setting forth the specific terms and conditions of the buy/sale transaction can help avoid costly and time-consuming disputes.

Why a Stock Purchase Instead of Another Form of Acquisition?

Stock Purchase Generally

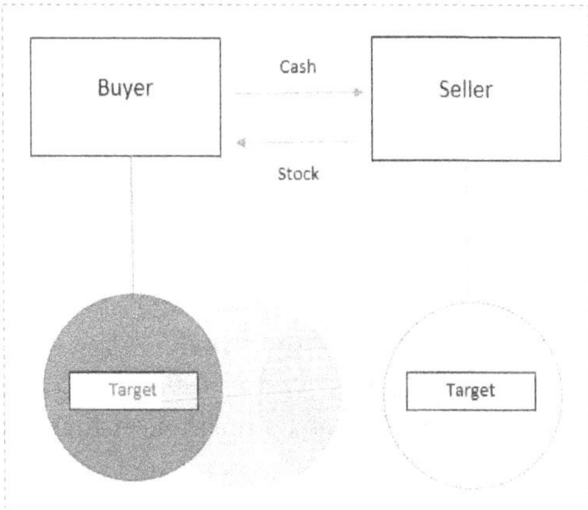

A stock purchase is perhaps the most common transaction structure used to buy and sell a privately held business. There are, however, other structures in which a business can be transferred from one party to another, such as an asset purchase or a merger. Transaction structure can be influenced by numerous issues, such as the parties' respective objectives and bargaining positions, tax matters, the structure in which the seller owns the business, the laws under which the seller and the business operate, the ultimate goals of the buyer and seller with respect to the transaction, and countless other issues. This book does not address all the issues that may dictate what transaction structure is best for a buyer or seller. Such a discussion is a worthy topic, but would justify one or more entirely separate books. A buyer and seller must work closely with their advisors to determine what transaction structure is optimal given their respective goals and the facts and circumstances surrounding the transaction. We will, however, address briefly the general pros and cons of a stock purchase, asset purchase, and merger structure to buy and sell a business.

In a stock purchase transaction, the buyer acquires all the outstanding stock of a company directly from its stockholders. Typically, the buyer uses cash as currency for acquiring the shares, but a buyer might instead use its stock as currency or a combination of its stock and cash. Under this transaction structure, if the buyer wishes to acquire all the target company's outstanding stock, the buyer must obtain agreement from all the target company stockholders to sell their shares to the buyer. This can sometimes be a daunting task for the buyer if there are numerous stockholders or if the stockholders are not in agreement among themselves that they should sell their shares or, if so, on what terms and conditions should they sell. After a stock purchase is complete, the target company continues to exist, but as a subsidiary of the buyer.

> **Author's Note**: If the target business is a limited liability company, a limited partnership or some other business entity, then the buyer would acquire membership interests, limited partnership interests, or the equity interests of such other business entity.

A transaction structured as a stock purchase can be viewed as advantageous to the buyer because it typically ensures that it will obtain the entire business. However, because the buyer is acquiring the entire business entity, a stock purchase can also be viewed as a disadvantage to a buyer if the business entity has liabilities that are unrelated to the business or are otherwise not desirable to the buyer in the future operation of the business. A buyer must conduct sufficient due diligence to ensure that all the assets used in the business are owned by the target company and that there are no liabilities of the target company that are unrelated to the business or undesirable from a go-forward perspective. A stock purchase transaction can be viewed as advantageous to both the buyer and seller in that the documentation is relatively simple—a stock purchase agreement, which is often coupled with a stock power recording the transfer of shares. Other transaction structures, such as an asset purchase, require various ancillary documents, such as deeds, bills of sale, and other instruments of transfer, to consummate the transaction.

Asset Purchase Generally

In an asset purchase, a buyer purchases some or all of the assets of a target company. Similar to stock purchase transaction, the buyer can use cash as currency to acquire the assets or can use a combination of its stock and cash. Unlike a stock purchase, the buyer deals directly with the seller (i.e., the target company), not its stockholders. After an asset purchase is consummated, the seller continues to exist, though where substantially all of its assets have been sold, the remaining entity generally has no residual value and is usually dissolved once its post-closing obligations under the definitive purchase agreement, if any, are satisfied. As a result, approval by the stockholders of the seller is typically required by law if substantially all of a seller's assets are sold to protect stockholders against the disposal of all of the seller's value without their consent.

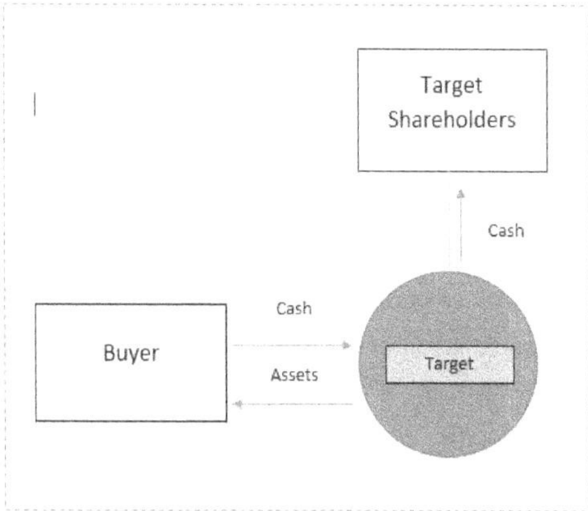

A transaction structured as asset purchase is typically seen as advantageous in the following ways: (1) the buyer can "cherry pick" only those assets it wishes to own and only those liabilities it agrees to assume; and (2) the buyer will receive a "stepped-up" basis in the assets acquired, which can provide a buyer with potential tax savings upon a subsequent sale of the assets.

On the other hand, an asset purchase may be seen as disadvantageous for the following reasons: (1) because the seller must transfer the purchased assets in piecemeal, the likelihood increases that an asset may be overlooked that is required for the buyer to continue operating the business as the seller did before the transfer; (2) where significant real

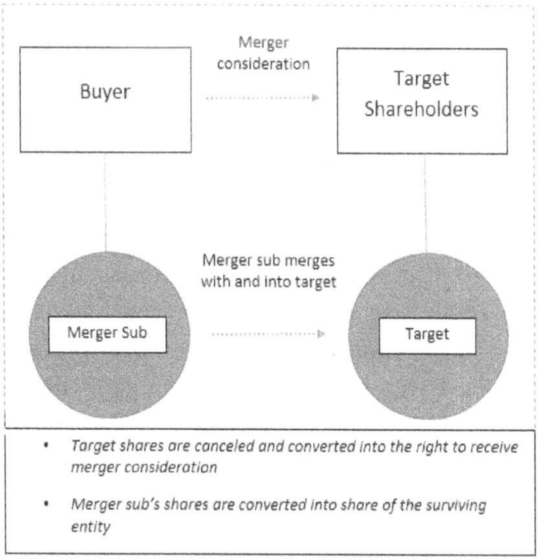

property is transferred, tax costs are likely to be high for the seller; (3) the buyer's ability to select assets to purchase and liabilities to assume, though valuable in some respects, may increase transaction costs because third-party consent is often required for transfer and may be difficult to secure; (4) buyers generally must take on all operating liabilities tied to the operating assets it purchases. Nonetheless, in some cases, a seller may be at a disadvantage where the buyer can negotiate the purchase of operating assets without having to assume the associated liabilities. As a result, the seller may be left with liabilities but no valuable assets with which to generate revenue to satisfy them. In a few cases, this arrangement may also be disadvantageous for the buyer under the doctrine of *de facto* merger. Under the *de facto* merger doctrine, in some states, a buyer who purchases substantially all of a seller's assets could be liable for tort damages associated with the purchased business that arose before the transaction occurred if certain facts exist. This legal doctrine could produce enormous and unpredictable liability for a buyer. Again, though asset purchases provide some perceived advantages, a buyer should evaluate all factors before settling on this structure.

Merger Generally

In a transaction structured as a merger, the target company is merged with an entity controlled by the buyer pursuant to state law. Several types of mergers exist, the most popular of which is a reverse subsidiary merger. In a reverse subsidiary merger, a subsidiary of the buyer mergers with and into the target company, with the target company surviving the merger. As a result of this transaction, and pursuant to state law, (1) the stock of the buyer merger subsidiary is converted into shares of the target company, and (2) the stock of the target company is cancelled and converted into the right either to receive merger consideration or to exercise statutory appraisal rights in court. The buyer succeeds to the target company's assets and liabilities by operation of law and by virtue of the target company becoming a wholly owned subsidiary of the buyer. State law usually requires that mergers be approved by the boards of directors of both constituent corporations and by the stockholders of the target company, and in some cases, the buyer. A merger is effectively a stock purchase for tax purposes because the buyer is deemed to have acquired all outstanding stock of the target company.

A merger transaction is typically seen as advantageous for the following reasons: (1) the buyer negotiates directly with the target company's management, instead of with each of the stockholders as in a stock purchase, which may simplify negotiation in some cases; (2) assets and liabilities are assumed in bulk by operation of law (similar to a stock purchase), instead of by individual transfer as in an asset purchase; again, this may simplify negotiation and reduce transaction costs; (3) mergers can be structured in a way that allows sellers to mitigate the income tax that might otherwise arise if the transaction were structured as a stock purchase or asset purchase; (4) a merger can be completed, and the target company combined with the buyer, over the objection of seller stockholders so long as minimum stockholder approval requirements are met, with some exceptions.

On the other hand, a transaction structured as a merger may be seen as disadvantageous because, similar to a stock purchase transaction, the buyer acquires the entire target company, including all of its assets and liabilities by operation of law, it runs significant risk of acquiring known but undesirable liabilities and unknown or undisclosed liabilities, which may reduce the value of the transaction or prove costly to the buyer after the transaction closes.

This brief overview of the advantages and drawbacks of the three basic acquisition structures shows that there is no one structure that is preferable in all, or even most, situations. Buyers and sellers should carefully consider their objectives for the transaction and other factors in both the ideal and practical sense, and seek legal, tax, and financial advice before settling on one structure over another.

Advantages and Disadvantages of M&A Structures

Structure	Advantages	Disadvantages
Stock	- Buyer acquires all the assets owned by the target. - Simple structure. - Does not trigger anti-assignment clauses in commercial contracts. - Typically does not trigger taxes on transfer of assets.	- Assumption of all liabilities, known and unknown. - Negotiations can be complicated if numerous stockholders. - Typically need 100% stockholder participation.

		- Might trigger "change of control" clauses in commercial contracts, which may give the other party a termination right.
Asset	- Buyer can "cherry pick" assets and leave behind undesirable liabilities. - Buyer receives "stepped-up" tax basis in assets.	- Buyer risks missing key assets. - Potential tax payment obligation for seller if significant real estate assets are transferred. - Typically triggers third party consents under commercial contracts being assigned to buyer. - Bulk sales laws apply in some states.
Merger	- Easier to negotiate with target's management. - Assets of target are assumed in bulk by operation of law - Allows "freeze out" of minority stockholders who oppose the transaction. - Tax efficient.	- Assumption of all liabilities, known and unknown. - Opposing stockholders may have dissenter/ appraisal rights.

What is the Typical Process for Buying and Selling a Business?

The complexity, time, and cost of the process for buying and selling a business can vary significantly from transaction to transaction based on numerous factors, including the size of the business, the structure in which the seller owns the business, the location of the business, the industry and regulatory regime in which the business operates, employee matters, the pre-existing relationship (or lack thereof) between the buyer and seller (whether as competitors or otherwise), and countless other issues. A successful transaction process usually culminates with the buyer and the seller entering into a definitive agreement for the purchase and sale of the business and subsequently closing the transaction under the terms of that agreement.

The Road to a Deal

General Overview

Whether you find yourself in a buyer- or seller-driven process, the road to a deal usually begins with the execution of a non-disclosure agreement and ends with the exchange of shares for cash in the case of a stock purchase. While the path between these two end points is varied depending on the particular details of a given transaction (no two deals are exactly the same), they generally take one of the two paths set forward below.

Table 1(a)

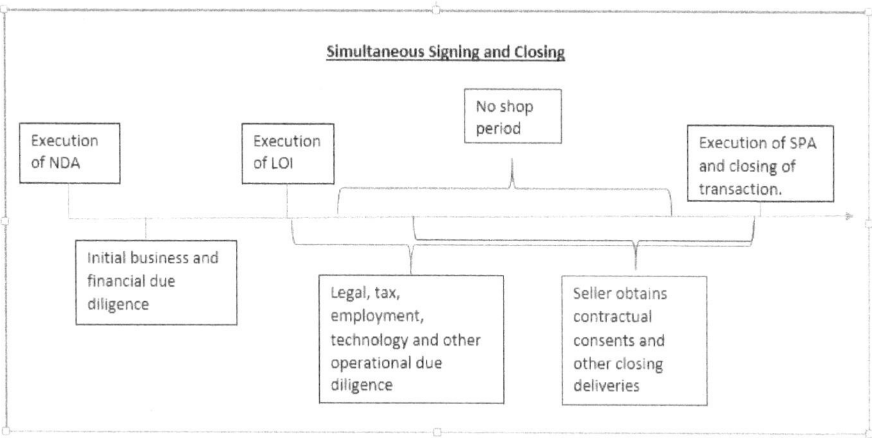

Table 1(b)

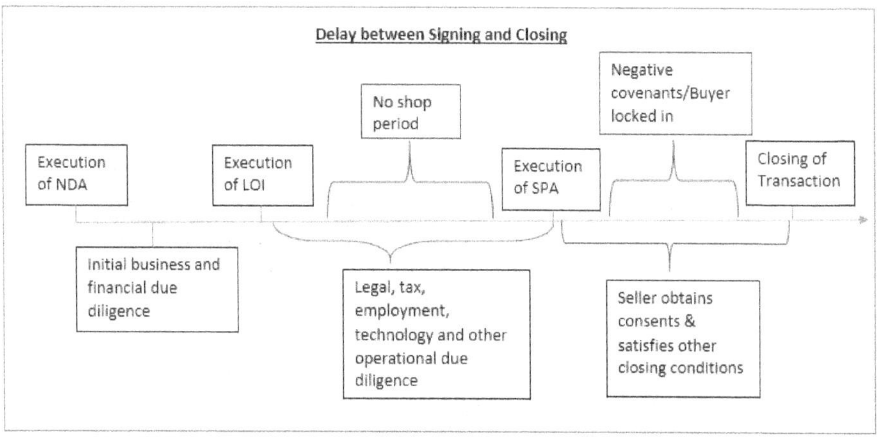

In both cases, after the parties execute a non-disclosure agreement protecting the proprietary information of the target company, the buyer begins its initial due diligence investigation of the target. The goal of this initial diligence phase is two-fold in nature: for the buyer (1) to determine operationally and strategically if the target business would be a good fit and (2) to value the target to determine its initial purchase price range. This is the first decision point where the buyer makes a "go/no go" decision.

The LOI

If after completing due diligence the buyer still wants to move forward with a transaction, it will have initial purchase price negotiations with the seller, that, if successful, will culminate in the parties executing a formal letter of intent, term sheet, or non-binding offer (customarily referred to as an LOI). While typically non-binding in nature, the purpose of the LOI is to set forth a preliminary agreement between buyer and seller on purchase price and other deal terms that will then form the framework on which the definitive agreement is constructed. An LOI will also usually have a "no-shop" covenant that requires the seller, for a certain period of time, to (i) negotiate a sale of the target (or any similar transaction) only with the prospective buyer and (ii) not entertain any similar acquisition offers from any other third parties. This provides the buyer with a certain level of comfort in light of the substantial investment of time and payment legal and third-party advisor fees the buyer will undertake in connection with its consideration of the deal. A sample "no-shop" covenant is set forth below.

> ***Sample "No–Shop" Covenant***
>
> ***In consideration of Buyer entering into this Letter of Intent and undertaking to investigate the businesses of the Company and to incur expenses in connection therewith, the Company and each Seller hereby agree that, until 5:00 p.m. Eastern Standard Time on that date certain ninety (90) days after the date hereof (the "No Shop Date"), neither the Company, the Sellers, nor any of their affiliates, officers, directors, employees, agents, or advisors shall, directly or indirectly, solicit or entertain offers from, negotiate with or in any manner encourage, discuss, accept, or consider any proposal of***

> ***any other person or entity relating to the acquisition of the stock or other securities of the Company or its assets or businesses, in whole or in part, through purchase, merger, consolidation, share exchange or otherwise, or any other business combination involving the Company. In addition, the Company and the Sellers agree immediately to cease and cause to be terminated any previously undertaken or ongoing activities, discussions or negotiations with any other person or entity with respect to any transaction of the type described in the preceding sentence. Furthermore, if the Company, the Sellers, or any of their affiliates, officers, directors, employees, agents, or advisors receives any communication regarding any offer or proposal of the type described in the first sentence of this Section between the date hereof and the No Shop Date, then the Company and the Sellers shall immediately notify Buyer of the receipt of such proposal and shall promptly provide to Buyer a copy of such proposal (or if such proposal is not in writing, a written summary of its terms).***

With the exception of sell-side auction deals (where a seller may negotiate simultaneously with two or more competing buyers until the definitive agreement is executed), it is customary for a buyer to demand that the seller agree to be bound by a "no–shop" covenant. The duration of the "no–shop" covenant is usually the most negotiated part of the covenant. On one hand, the buyer will want this to be as long as possible to protect its substantial investment of time and third-party advisor fees it will incur in connection with conducting due diligence and drafting and negotiating the transaction documents. The seller, on the other hand, will want this restriction on considering alternative transactions with other suitors to be as short as possible given that there is no guarantee of a deal with buyer. Generally, the parties settle somewhere between thirty and ninety days, occasionally where extensions are subject to the completion of certain milestones.

Due Diligence

Once the LOI is executed, the buyer will begin its full diligence investigation of the target company. From a legal perspective the primary goals of diligence are

(1) to identify any major legal issues that might affect the valuation of the business or interfere or otherwise restrict the buyer's ownership or operation of the business post-closing; and (2) to identify required consents and approvals that will be required in connection with the transaction. In doing this, the buyer's attorney will want to review and analyze all of the target company's (and its subsidiary's) constitutional documents, minutes of stockholders and board meetings, capitalization table, stock ledgers, financial statements, permits, leases, licenses and other contracts, court documents regarding pending litigation, settlement agreements, correspondence with governmental agencies, tax returns and other tax documents, employee benefits plans and related documents, information regarding employees and contractors, intellectual property filings and other documents and titles for owned real estate. A detailed step-by-step instruction of due diligence is outside the scope of this book, but set forth below are some of the critical due diligence items a buyer should consider when conducting due diligence on a target company.

Diligence Big Ticket Items:

- Start by reviewing the minutes of the company's board and stockholders meetings and current financial statements to get an overview of the business and operations of the target and potential legal contingencies.
- Google the company to ensure no material adverse results in at least the first ten pages.
- Check with the secretary of state and ensure that the target is in good standing in its jurisdiction of formation.
- Run UCC checks on the target and its founders.
- Run pacer litigation checks on the target and its founders. Make sure any pending litigation would not, if determined adversely to the company, affect the ability of the target to operate its business in the ordinary course (e.g., no pending litigation regarding the validity of key target intellectual property).
- Review contracts for change of control provisions, term and termination provisions, IP assignment clauses, non-compete agreements, and most-favored nation pricing clauses.
- Review chain of title for any owned real property and consider phase I and II environmental reports.
- Check chain of title on all key company intellectual property. Start by confirming that all contractors and employees have executed non-disclosure and invention assignment agreements.

A seller usually also conducts its own due diligence on its company (often refered to as "reverse diligence") to uncover any "surprises" before the buyer does so in its due diligence investigation of the business. If a seller uncovers any material liabilities in "reverse diligence", it is common (and a good practice) for that seller to bring such findings to the buyer's attention promptly. This allows the seller to control the manner in which the potentially negative information is presented to the buyer, and reassures the buyer of the seller's credibility. It is always far worse when a seller tries to cover up a risk or liability and waits for the buyer to find it in its diligence investigation. When this happens, the buyer may start asking what else the seller is hiding, which may amplify the perceived impact of any unexpected potential liability that was discovered. In a worst-case scenario, a buyer may lose all confidence in the seller and walk away from the deal. After all, the representations and warranties in a purchase agreement are only as good as a seller's credibility and creditworthiness. This brings us to a question that many clients may ask: "Why do we need to spend all this money on due diligence when we have protection in the representations and warranties and indemnities?" The answer is that due diligence is, among other things, the buyer's opportunity to detect liabilities while the purchase price is still in the buyer's bank account. If a buyer seeks to recover purchase price post-closing through indemnification for a breach of a representation or warranty, it must make the seller (often through litigation) disgorge the cash. This can be a long drawn-out, time-consuming, and expensive process without any certainty of success. Additionally, the seller may no longer have any cash remaining at the end of this process, as it may have spent it all by the time the buyer realized it had an indemnification claim.

If the buyer uncovers any material liability in due diligence, then there are three likely potential outcomes: (1) for unconditional liabilities or contingent liabilities that can be quantified, the buyer will likely request a purchase price reduction; (2) for contingent liabilities that are difficult to quantify, the buyer will likely request that the seller indemnify the buyer for amount of liability actually incurred post-closing (assuming that the estimated amount of the liability is small relative to the overall transaction value) and (3) if the estimated amount of the liability is so large or unpredictable that it outweighs the benefits of the transaction, the parties may determine that it is best to call off the deal or put it on hold until the parties are able to come to some mutually agreeable solution regarding the treatment of the liability.

Timing of Signing and Closing

Assuming that following diligence the buyer decides to go forward with a transaction, a stock purchase agreement will generally be structured one of two ways, as set forth in Tables 1(a) and 1(b) above. The first of these is a simultaneous signing and closing—meaning the parties execute the stock purchase agreement and exchange stock for consideration on the same date. This should be compared to a purchase agreement that is structured with a delay between signing and closing, where the parties sign the purchase agreement on one date but do not close until days, weeks, or months later once all the conditions to closing have been satisfied.

There are various reasons that the parties might desire to sign the purchase agreement on one day and have some time pass before they close the deal. For example, there may be contingencies discovered in due diligence that the buyer requires the seller to resolve prior to closing, but wants the seller to commit to selling on specific terms in the mean time. But more often than not, this delay is driven by third-party consents—either government consents or contractual consent. The buyer will typically demand that the seller seek and obtain a contractual consent when (i) the target company is a party to a commercial contract (customer contract, supply contract, lease agreement, or other contract necessary to operate the business in the same manner as seller), which the buyer desires to maintain the benefit of post-closing, and (ii) the contract gives the other party the right to terminate the contract if the target company is no longer owned by the seller or otherwise requires the target company to obtain the other party's consent to the potential transaction , which if not obtained gives the other party a right to terminate the contract. Governmental consents typically arise as a matter of law, that is, the law requires the party to obtain the consent of a certain governmental entity before consummating the transaction, which if not obtained would be illegal and subject the parties to potential fines, penalties and other government action. The most common governmental consents are those that arise under anti-trust and anti-competition laws (such as Hart-Scott-Rodino), which generally come into play due to the value of the transaction or the relative market share controlled by the buyer and the seller. In the case of both contractual consents and governmental consents, for one reason or another, the parties want the certainty of a signed contract prior to taking any further action. However, in this case, the corollary of certainty is commitment, in that once the parties have executed the definitive agreement, they must close the deal unless the other party fails to comply with one of the closing conditions set forth in the agreement (e.g., the seller fails to obtain material contractual consents, the parties do not obtain governmental approval, either party does not perform its covenants that are required to be performed prior to closing, or the target company suffers a material adverse change.). Further, between the signing and closing, the target company will be bound by certain restrictive covenants that require it to act in the ordinary course of business and restrict it from taking certain actions, such as paying dividends, selling assets, altering benefits plans, increasing employee compensation, or otherwise taking any action that could adversely affect the value of the target company.

Sample Change of Control Provision

Neither party shall assign or transfer any of its rights or obligations under this agreement, by operation of law or otherwise, without the prior written consent of the other party; provided, that, so there may be no doubt, a change in the ownership of 50% or more of the capital stock of a party shall be deemed to be an assignment for purposes of this section.

Certain Transaction Assumptions

As you can see from the above, a transaction structured as a stock purchase can be very complex. For instructional purposes and simplicity's sake, we have made the following assumptions in this agreement:

- Each party is a corporation formed under the laws of Delaware.
- The target business is housed in a Delaware corporation, which is wholly owned by the seller.
- All of the assets and liabilities of the target corporation arise from or relate to the operation of the business.
- The target company owns all the assets required to operate the business.
- The target corporation has no subsidiaries.
- No third party approvals are required (whether as a result of contracts or governmental approvals, such as Hart-Scott-Rodino).
- Buyer does not require any debt financing to obtain funds to pay the purchase price (buyer is paying the purchase price with cash on hand).

- The target corporation does not have any indebtedness and there are no payment contingencies that are triggered in connection with the transaction.
- The only outstanding equity securities of the target company are the shares of capital stock that the buyer is purchasing from the seller, in other words, there are no outstanding warrants, stock options or other equity securities exercisable for, or convertible into, shares of the target company's capital stock.

Guest Note on Deal Negotiation Basics by Shawn K. Baldwin, Senior Vice President and Group Counsel at Equifax, Inc.

- **Two Schools**. Generally there are two schools of thought on negotiating M&A deal terms. One school, a more traditional approach, favors initially taking positions that are most favorable to your client (but often far from "market") with the hope that after everything washes out in negotiations your client will end up with more deal points in their favor. This approach can be very effective where one party is sophisticated and the other is not, or if negotiating leverage is skewed. But when both parties are working from a level playing field this approach tends to result in time-consuming and expensive negotiations, and can potentially negatively affect the relationship among the parties. The alternative is to start out in the middle of the road (or relatively close to the middle of the road) and take principled positions based on the particular facts and circumstances of the transaction (e.g., line item indemnification or carve outs for specific operational risks detected in diligence). While this latter approach is more reasonable and even handed, it carries the risk that the counterparty takes the first approach and uses your principled position as the starting point for zero sum negotiations.

- **Deal studies**. There are a number of institutions such as the American Bar Association and Houlihan Lokey that prepare statistical summaries of deal points for transactions closed in a particular year. These studies provide survey information such as the mean and median basket, caps, carve outs, escrows and other material deal terms for reported M&A transactions. These statistics can be very useful when attempting to gain consensus on what is "customary" or "market". However, it should be noted that deal studies can be a double-edged blade. If you make an argument based on a deal study you are essentially validating that deal study in its entirety, so be prepared for the other party to push for other terms set forth in the study which may be less favorable to your client.

- **Who has the pen**. Customarily, with the exception of auctions (where form purchase agreements are served up by the sellers), the purchaser is responsible for the first draft of the purchase agreement. Hence the term "purchaser's paper". That said, a pro-active seller may attempt to beat purchaser to the punch and produce the first draft of the purchase agreement so that they benchmark the starting place for negotiations.

- **Horse trading**. Expect the negotiation of the transaction in its final hours to get down to a handfull of essential deal terms. With this in mind it is often helpful to reserve some issues that you think will be important to the other side for use as currency in last-minute trading.

- **Publicly Disclosed Precedent.** When dealing with a publicly traded counterparty it can be advantageous to search their SEC filings for past deals to see what they agreed to in previous transactions.

Line-by-Line Analysis

Preamble and Recitals

Found near the very beginning of the agreement, the preamble and recitals set the stage of the transaction by describing the players and the general gist of who is transferring what to whom. This section is often viewed by many attorneys as mere boiler plate; however, courts typically view this section as statements of fact. An enterprising attorney; therefore, will see this as an opportunity, thinking of worst-case scenario, to talk to the court (or arbitrator) and explain to them in layperson's terms what is going on with the deal, who is involved, what consideration is being paid, and what is being purchased. In doing so, you should consider whether there are any other commercial agreements that are tied to the transaction or that the transaction is conditioned upon. For example, is there going to be one or more ancillary agreements that will be executed simultaneous with the closing, which are meaningful to the overall transaction, such as non-competition agreements, transition services agreements or other commercial arrangements?

> **Author's Note**: A more in-depth discussion of non-competition agreements can be found in Section 6.04.

The recitals typically also include the definition of the target business. This is important because it plays through the entirety of the agreement and informs the scope of the representations and warranties set forth in Articles III and IV of the agreement. Depending on the particular agreement, it may also tie into the non-compete agreement. Accordingly, it is very important for both parties that this definition be as accurate as possible. Out of an abundance of caution, the buyer will typically default to a broader, all-encompassing definition of the target business. A seller, on the other hand, will not want the definition of the business to be narrow in scope so that it will not have to represent or warrant to anything outside the scope of the actual business and how it is currently owned and operated.

THIS STOCK PURCHASE AGREEMENT, dated [_________ ___, 20__] (the "Closing Date"), is made and entered into by and between [Buyer], a Delaware

corporation (the "Buyer"), and [Seller], a Delaware corporation (the "Seller"). The Buyer and the Seller are sometimes referred to individually in this Agreement as a "Party" and collectively as the "Parties."

RECITALS

A. [Target Company], a Delaware corporation (the "Company"), is engaged in the business of [__________] (the "Business").
B. The Seller owns all the Company's issued and outstanding shares of capital stock (the "Company Shares").
C. The Parties desire to enter into this Agreement pursuant to which the Seller will sell to the Buyer, and the Buyer will purchase from the Seller, all the Company Shares on the terms and subject to the conditions set forth herein (the "Acquisition").
D. Upon the consummation of the transactions contemplated by this Agreement, including the Acquisition (collectively, the "Transactions"), the Buyer will own all the Company Shares.
E. The Parties desire to make certain representations, warranties, covenants and other agreements in connection with the foregoing as specified herein.

AGREEMENT

In consideration of the foregoing and the respective representations, warranties, covenants, agreements and conditions set forth in this Agreement, and intending to be legally bound by this Agreement, the Parties agree as follows:

ARTICLE I
ACQUISITION AND PURCHASE PRICE MATTERS

Article I covers the fundamental details of the stock purchase transaction. It sets forth the specific terms of the transfer of the shares, the amount of the purchase price, and how the purchase price will be paid. Accordingly, the parties must pay close attention to details of this section when drafting.

Section 1.01 makes clear that the buyer is paying for, and receiving, the shares of the target company's capital stock owned by the seller, free and clear of all liens. This means that the shares have no encumbrances so they are freely transferrable and the seller is not, and buyer will not be, subject to any prohibition on transfer or any sort of liens or other impediments on the value of those shares. This section also makes clear that the closing of the transfer is simultaneous with the signing of the agreement. If there were a delay between signing and closing, this language would specify that the transfer would take place at the "closing."

> **Section 1.01 Purchase and Sale. Subject to the terms and conditions of this Agreement, <u>contemporaneously with the execution and delivery</u> of this Agreement by the Parties, the Seller hereby sells, transfers and delivers to the Buyer, and the Buyer hereby purchases and acquires from the Seller, all the Company Shares, <u>free and clear of all Liens</u>, in exchange for the Buyer's payment of the Purchase Price pursuant to Section 1.02.**

Section 1.02 sets forth the purchase price that the buyer is paying for the shares of the target company's capital stock. The transaction structure contemplated by this agreement is very simple—cash for shares. In more complex deals, you often see adjustments to the purchase price, such as deductions for the closing date indebtedness of the target company, transaction expenses incurred by the target company and its stockholders (such as amounts owed to investment bankers), and payments owed to employees for severance, transaction bonuses or other payments due as a result of the transaction. Additionally, there may be other adjustments to the purchase price to reflect the economic deal agreed to by the buyer and the seller.

Guest Note on Purchase Price Valuation by Ethan Thompson, Director, New Initiatives, Product Management at McKesson Corporation

It is often said that valuation is an art, not a science. There is no "correct answer" when determining the value of a company. In the end, the accuracy depends on the quality of the information available and ultimately how the business performs in the future. The goal is to distill all available data into a "best estimate" of value and use this as a benchmark to negotiate a purchase price that provides financially acceptable returns. There are many available methodologies available to perform a valuation, varying in complexity from rules of thumb to multi-month financial exercises. Below are a few of the more common methodologies used in the market.

1) **Discounted Cash Flow (DCF)** – In the DCF analysis a business case is developed to project future cash flows based on a set of operating assumptions. The projected cash flows are then discounted to give their present values — the sum of all future cash flows, both incoming and outgoing, is the net present value (NPV). The discount rate used is based on risk and required return to the investor. This methodology is the de facto standard to determine value, but is limited by the quality/accuracy of the business case developed.
2) **Transaction Comparables** – This method uses past completed transactions in the market as a comparative tool to estimate the value of future transactions. This is practical when comparing companies in similar markets, or with similar service offerings/business models. Typically the reference multiples used are Revenue-to-Price or Profit-to-Price. For example: if Acme Inc was sold for $100M two years ago and had $250M of revenue and $20M of profit, they would have a Revenue-to-Price multiple of 2.5x and an EBITDA-to-Profit multiple of 5.0x. These multiples could then be used to approximate a price range for the company being sold. This is practical as a benchmarking tool to determine a range of possible value.
3) **Market Comparables** – Similar to transaction comparables, this methodology uses financial ratios to estimate value. The comparison is to public companies in similar markets, or with similar service offerings/business models. Typically the reference multiples used are Revenue-to-Value or Profit-to-Value. The "Value" metric is based on the enterprise value of the public company. The benefit of using this methodology is the availability of public data. The end result often ends in a wide range of value estimates and is practical as a benchmarking tool.

> **Section 1.02 Purchase Price. In consideration for the Company Shares, the Buyer shall pay, or cause to be paid, at the Closing, an amount in cash equal to [______ Dollars ($•)] (the "Purchase Price"). After the Closing, the Purchase Price shall be subject to adjustment in accordance with Section 7.08 (Indemnification).**

As you can see from the last sentence, any claims made pursuant to claims for indemnification are treated as an adjustment to purchase price. It is not uncommon to also see post-closing net working capital adjustments to purchase price. These so-called "net working capital adjustments" are based on the assumption that the target company will have a certain historically normalized level of working capital at closing to enable buyer to run the business just as the seller did prior to the closing. This historically normalized amount (a net working capital target) is usually determined by accountants by reference to the target company's past financial statements. Any amounts in excess of this target (a net working capital surplus) should be distributed by the buyer to the seller and amounts below the target (a net working capital deficit) should be paid by the seller to the buyer, in each case, at or after the closing of the transaction.

> **Author's Note**: Net working capital is an indicator of a company's ability to meet its short-term debts in the ordinary course of business. It is calculated by subtracting the company's current liabilities from its current assets. Parties will usually agree on net working capital guidelines that set forth which balance sheet accounts will be included in current assets and liabilities and may even have a sample calculation of net working capital.

This usually occurs by way of an informal audit process where the buyer prepares a preliminary net working capital schedule following the closing and provides it to the seller. The seller then has the opportunity to review and to dispute such schedule. Eventually, the schedule is finalized by the agreement of the parties, or failing that, a third-party accountant. Below is a sample provision. Please note that this particular clause has a "basket" or "band" where no payment is made unless the deficit or surplus exceeds the target by a certain denominated amount.

Sample Net Working Capital Provision

Purchase Price Adjustment.

(a) Within [one hundred and twenty (120) calendar days] following the Closing Date, [Buyer] shall deliver to the Sellers a statement of the Net Working Capital of the Business as of the Closing Date (the "Preliminary Net Working Capital Statement"). "Net Working Capital" shall mean (x) the aggregate amount of the current assets of the Company, minus (y) the aggregate amount of the current liabilities of the Company, each determined in accordance with the guidelines set forth on Schedule 1.03(a) hereto.

Note: The duration of the period of time post-closing and whether the buyer or the sellers are responsible for preparing the preliminary net working capital statement are often subject to negotiation among the parties.

(b) If within thirty (30) calendar days following the delivery of the Preliminary Net Working Capital Statement, the Sellers have not given Buyer written notice of objection to such Preliminary Net Working Capital Statement identifying with particularity the Sellers' grounds for objection and its alternative calculation of Net Working Capital (such notice, the "Notice of Objection"), the Preliminary Net Working Capital Statement shall be deemed to be the Final Net Working Capital Statement and shall be final and binding on all parties. If the Sellers deliver a Notice of Objection within such time period, then the Parties shall use their commercially reasonable efforts to attempt to resolve the issues raised in such Notice of Objection. If the Parties are unable to resolve such matter within 30 days following receipt by Buyer of the Notice of Objection, then the issues remaining in dispute shall be submitted to [Ernst & Young] (the "Independent Accounting Firm") for final resolution

applying the practices set forth in the Net Working Capital guidelines. The decision issued by the Independent Accounting Firm shall be final and binding on the parties hereto. All fees and expenses relating to the work of the Independent Accounting Firm shall be borne by Buyer, on the one hand, and by Sellers, on the other hand, in inverse proportion as they may prevail on the matters resolved by the Independent Accounting Firm, which allocation shall be determined by the Independent Accounting Firm at the time the determination of the Independent Accounting Firm is rendered on the merits of the matters submitted to it. For purposes of this Agreement, (x) "<u>Final Working Capital Statement</u>" means the Net Working Capital Statement as finally determined pursuant to this Section 1.03(b) and (y) "<u>Target Working Capital</u>" shall mean an amount equal to [$●].

Note: It is generally advisable to select a particular third-party accountant for resolution of disputes in the purchase agreement. If post-closing net working capital discussions require third-party resolution post-closing, it is unlikely that the parties will be able to expeditiously agree on a neutral at that time.

(c) On or before the fifth (5th) Business Day following the determination of the Final Working Capital Statement pursuant to Section 1.03(b),

(i) if Net Working Capital as set forth on the Final Working Capital Statement is at least [$●] less than Target Working Capital, then the Sellers shall pay over to Buyer, a cash amount equal to the difference between (x) the Net Working Capital as set forth on the Final Working Capital Statement and (y) the Target Working Capital.

> ***(ii) if, on the other hand, Net Working Capital as set forth on the Final Working Capital Statement [exceeds the Target Working Capital by at least [$•]), then Buyer shall pay over to the Sellers, a cash amount equal to the difference between (x) the Net Working Capital as set forth on the Final Working Capital Statement and (y) the Target Working Capital.***

Note: As noted above, this particular provision has a dollar basket. This means that no payment must be made by a party unless the amount owed is greater than the amount of the basket. Parties will typically negotiate such a basket to avoid a party making a payment that is not material in amount.

One last purchase price adjustment worth discussing is an "earn out." An earn out is a performance-based mechanic that is used to bridge the gap between the buyer's and the seller's respective valuations of the target business. Usually it comes into play where the seller projects a much higher revenue growth rate for the target business than the buyer, resulting in a valuation gap. To find a compromise position, the buyer will sometimes agree to pay a base purchase price at closing and then pay additional amounts post-closing if the company achieves certain revenue or EBITDA (earnings before interest tax depreciation and amortization) targets. Earn outs have grown into disfavor in recent years as a result of a change of accounting treatment that requires a buyer to record the fair value of the earn out at closing and adjust periodically post-closing based on the likelihood of payment. The buyer should use special care in drafting earn out provisions as they are often a hot bed for post-closing disputes. If the target company fails to achieve set earn out targets, the seller may allege that such failure was a result of one or more decisions made by the buyer in bad faith or with the intent to suppress revenue or unduly increase cost and thus fall short of the earn out target.

ARTICLE II
CLOSING DELIVERIES AND ACTIONS

Article II sets forth a blue print of exactly what is going to occur at the closing and the deliverables for which each party is responsible. Section 2.01

establishes the timing of when and the location of where the closing will occur. As you will note, the parties may elect to have a virtual closing or meet at a location to exchange the closing documents. While in-person closings are still common in some regions of the world, where they are often followed by small celebrations, in the United States virtual closings are customary. Regardless of whether an in-person or virtual closing is selected, it is good practice to organize and account for all the required closing deliverables the day before the selected closing date. This means executing all ancillary documents and delivering them to the other party, together with all other closing deliverables, to be held in escrow until the delivering party authorizes their release. This is generally the desired mechanic for closing so that all each party needs to do on the closing date at the closing is to confirm that its has received from the other party all the closing documents that the other party was required to deliver pursuant to the definitive agreement. If that is the case, all that needs to be completed is the payment of the purchase price, which typically occurs by way of bank wire transfer of same day funds.

> **Section 2.01 Closing. The consummation of the Acquisition (the "Closing") shall take place contemporaneously with the execution and delivery of this Agreement by the Parties and shall occur either (a) remotely by the exchange of signature pages hereto and the delivery of those documents described in Section 2.02 and Section 2.03 by courier, facsimile or e-mail, and the performance of those actions described in Section 2.02 and Section 2.03, or (b) at such other time and place as the Parties may agree in writing signed by both Parties.**

Section 2.02 sets forth the documents and other items which the seller must deliver to the buyer at closing.

> **Section 2.02 Seller Closing Deliveries and Contemporaneous Actions. Contemporaneously with the execution and delivery of this Agreement, the Seller shall deliver, or cause to be delivered, to the Buyer the following:**

(a) stock certificates representing the Company Shares and accompanying stock powers duly executed by the Seller, evidencing the transfer of the Company Shares to the Buyer;

The seller must deliver to the buyer the actual stock certificates representing the target company shares, and such certificates must be endorsed on the back by the seller because they are not bearer shares where physical control is tantamount to ownership. The transfer should also be perfected on the books and records of the target company indicating that the buyer is the new record owner of the shares and removing the seller from the stockholder register. The buyer's counsel will want to carefully inventory each share certificate delivered at closing and compare it to the target company's stock register to ensure that certificates representing all the target company's issued and outstanding shares of capital stock are delivered.

(b) a certificate of the Secretary or any Assistant Secretary of the Company, dated as of the Closing Date, certifying that: (i) the Company's Organizational Documents, as attached thereto, are true, correct, and complete as of immediately prior to the Closing; (ii) the Company is in good standing in its jurisdiction of formation and in each other jurisdiction where it is qualified to do business, and attached thereto a good standing certificate of the Company, dated no more than thirty (30) days prior to the Closing Date; and (iii) each officer of the Company executing any Company Ancillary Document has been duly elected, has been qualified and, as of the Closing Date, is an officer of the Company holding the respective offices set opposite his or her name on such certificate and the

> **What is a certificate of good standing?** This is a document issued by the secretary of state of a company's state of incorporation. It verifies that the company truly exists, has paid all fees due to the secretary of state, and has completed the annual registration.

signature set opposite his or her name thereon is his or her genuine signature;

Generally referred to as a "secretary's certificate," this document gives the buyer additional comfort that they have been provided with true and accurate copies of the target company's organizational documents, the company is in good standing, and the representatives of the company are duly authorized to execute any documents for which they are responsible. There was a time when the legal trend was to have the seller's legal counsel deliver a formal opinion regarding these matters; however, such practice has fallen out of fashion.

(c) the Company's organizational record books, minute books and corporate seal; and

The buyer, as new owner of the company, will need to have possession of all the organizational records and minute books so that it can start maintaining them.

(d) a certificate duly completed and executed, dated as of the Closing Date and prepared in accordance with the requirements of U.S. Treasury Regulation sections 1.897-2(h) and 1.1445-2(c)(3), sufficient to establish that an interest in the Company held by a foreign person does not constitute a U.S. real property interest for purposes of Sections 897 and 1445 of the Code.

The buyer's counsel requires this certificate to ensure the seller is not a foreign person for purposes of the applicable regulation, which requires the buyer to withhold a portion of the purchase price attributable to the subject real estate. There seems to be some uncertainty among practitioners as to whether the applicable regulation applies to both leased and owned real property. Accordingly, the best practice is to ask for the certificate regardless of whether the target company leases or owns its property.

Section 2.03 sets forth the documents and other items which the buyer must deliver to the seller at closing.

Section 2.03 Buyer Closing Deliveries and Contemporaneous Actions. Contemporaneous with the execution and delivery of this Agreement, the Buyer shall:

(a) pay, or cause to be paid, to the Seller, the Purchase Price by wire transfer of immediately available funds to an account identified to the Buyer in writing by the Seller no fewer than two (2) Business Days prior to the Closing Date; and

Note that the purchase price is to be paid by bank wire transfer. This is generally due to the large sum of money that makes up the purchase price. One of the repercussions of requiring the purchase price to be paid by wire transfer is that the transaction must be closed on a business day within the hours set forth by the bank for wire transfers. Accordingly, it is good practice for buyer's counsel to call the buyer's bank and ascertain how late in the business day can the bank initiate a wire transfer that will arrive in the seller's account on that same day. Closings can, however, be held on non-banking days (e.g., when the parties want to close on a non-banking day because it is the end of an accounting period), but if the purchase price is a large amount, then the parties will need to think creatively given that banks often will not issue cashier's checks above a certain amount.

(b) deliver, or cause to be delivered, to the Seller, a certificate of the Secretary or any Assistant Secretary of the Buyer, dated as of the Closing Date, certifying that: (i) the Buyer is in good standing in its jurisdiction of formation and in each other jurisdiction where it is qualified to do business, and attached thereto a good standing certificate of the Buyer, dated no more than thirty (30) days prior to the Closing Date; and (ii) each officer of the Buyer executing any Buyer Ancillary Document has been duly elected, has been qualified and, as of the Closing Date, is an officer of the Buyer holding the respective offices set opposite his or her name on such certificate and

the signature set opposite his or her name thereon is his or her genuine signature.

This is the same as the certificate for the company set forth in 2.02(b).

ARTICLE III
SELLER REPRESENTATIONS & WARRANTIES

Author's Note on Representations & Warranties Generally: Articles III, IV, and V set forth certain representations and warranties of the parties. Generally speaking, representations and warranties are guaranties of certain statements of fact with respect to the target company and the business. These can be written positively or negatively (e.g. "the Company has been in full compliance with all applicable laws for the last five (5) years" or, alternatively, "the Company has not been in violation or breach of any applicable law during the last five (5) years"). Either way, they are generally drafted in absolutes with any exceptions set out on a schedule that corresponds to the section number of the applicable representation.

The seller's representations and warranties in a stock purchase agreement perform three primary functions:

(1) they set a baseline for seller's post-closing liability, which can occur if any of its representations or warranties are untrue or otherwise inaccurate;
(2) they confirm the buyer's due diligence investigation of the target company and the business, in that the buyer will typically request the seller to represent and warrant around basic matters as well as those uncovered by the buyer in its due diligence investigation of the target company and the business; and
(3) where the agreement is structured with a delay between signing and closing, they usually serve as (a) a condition to the buyer's obligation to close the transaction (that is, they must be true and accurate at the time of closing to obligate the buyer to close the transaction), and (b) a means by which the buyer can terminate the agreement prior to closing (that is, any of seller's representations or warranties becomes untrue or otherwise inaccurate and the seller does not cure it, then the buyer has a right to terminate the agreement.

Article III sets forth the representations and warranties of the seller. These representations are generally given with respect to the seller itself and not the company (as opposed to the representations and warranties in Article IV regarding the company). As such, when there is more than one seller, these reps are traditionally given severally and not jointly.

> **The Seller hereby represents and warrants to the Buyer as follows as of the Closing Date:**
>
> **Section 3.01 Authorization. The Seller has the right, power and capacity to (a) execute and deliver this Agreement and each Seller Ancillary Document, (b) perform the Seller's obligations under this Agreement and each Seller Ancillary Document, and (c) consummate the transactions contemplated this Agreement and each Seller Ancillary Document. The execution and delivery of this Agreement and each Seller Ancillary Document by the Seller, the performance by the Seller of its obligations hereunder and thereunder, and the consummation of the transactions provided for herein and therein, in each case, have been duly and validly authorized by the Seller. This Agreement and each Seller Ancillary Document has been duly executed and delivered by the Seller and each of them constitutes the valid and binding agreement of the Seller, enforceable against the Seller in accordance with their respective terms, subject to applicable bankruptcy, insolvency, reorganization, moratorium or other similar Laws affecting the enforcement of creditors' rights generally, general equitable principles and the discretion of courts in granting equitable remedies.**

This is a fundamental representation that you will find in almost every commercial transaction. It basically says the seller has the authority to undertake the transaction and to sign all the documents and perform all the obligations that are required to get the deal done. If a seller had any issue with giving this representation, then the buyer should have significant concern.

Section 3.02 Absence of Restrictions and Conflicts. The execution and delivery of this Agreement and the Seller Ancillary Documents, the consummation of the transactions contemplated hereby and thereby and the fulfillment of and compliance with the terms and conditions hereof and thereof do not or will not (as the case may be), with the passing of time or the giving of notice or both, (a) conflict with, result in any breach of, constitute a default (or an event that, with notice or lapse of time or both, would become a default) under, require any approval, consent or authorization of any Person pursuant to, or give to others any rights of termination, acceleration or cancellation of, any Contract, permit, franchise, license or other instrument applicable to the Seller, (b) conflict with or violate any Order to which the Seller is a party or by which the Seller or any of its properties are bound or (c) conflict with or violate any Law applicable to the Seller.

Like Section 3.01, this representation also falls into the category of "fundamental representations" that can be found in most commercial transactions. While Section 3.01 is focused on the seller's compliance with internal governance procedures, Section 3.02 is focused on seller's compliance with obligations borne by its interactions with third parties. This representation and warranty basically states that the execution of the stock purchase agreement and consummation of the transaction contemplated therein will not violate any contractual or other obligation to which the seller is a party or violate any law. Typically, a seller will attempt to negotiate some sort of materiality threshold for a breach of this representation and warranty so that it can avoid "foot fault" breaches.

Section 3.03 Ownership of Company Shares.

(a) The Seller has good and valid title to and beneficial ownership of all the Company Shares, and all the Company Shares are (i) validly issued, fully paid, and nonassessable, and (ii) free and clear of all Liens other than restrictions on transfer under state and federal securities Laws.

This representation and warranty ensures the buyer that the seller owns the shares and has a right to transfer them, that the shares are fully paid and are not subject to any encumbrances. This representation and warranty should be read in conjunction with the company rep regarding capitalization set forth in Section 4.03.

> "**Non-assessable**" means that the company cannot legally require the stockholder to make any further investments in the company. This should be contrasted with "assessable" shares where the company can require such additional contributions.

(b) Other than the Company Shares, the Seller does not own any shares of capital stock or other equity interests in the Company, or any option, warrant, right, call, commitment or right of any kind to have any shares of capital stock or other equity interests in the Company.

Section 3.03(b) states that the company shares that the seller is selling are the only securities in the target company that the seller owns. A buyer does not want to purchase 100 percent of the outstanding shares of common stock for at a valuation that assumes 100 percent ownership only to learn that the seller owns options that were not purchased by buyer or canceled in connection with the transaction.

Section 3.04 Legal Proceedings. There are no Actions pending or, to the knowledge of the Seller, threatened against, relating to or involving the Seller which could reasonably be expected to adversely affect the Seller's ability to consummate the Transactions or the transactions contemplated by the Seller Ancillary Documents.

Section 3.04 is a representation and warranty regarding outstanding litigation involving the seller. This representation and warranty should be distinguished from Section 4.04 regarding target company litigation. Essentially, this representation and warranty is the seller's affirmative statement that there does not exist any litigation or other legal actions involving the company shares or that otherwise could reasonably be expected to impede or interfere with the seller's transfer of shares to buyer. If any such litigation or legal actions exist, then the seller must disclose them to the buyer.

> **Section 3.05 Brokers, Finders and Investment Bankers. The Buyer will not be directly or indirectly obligated to pay or bear (e.g., by virtue of any payment by or obligation of the Seller at or at any time after the Closing) any brokerage, finder's or other fee or commission to any broker, finder or investment banker in connection with the Transactions or any of the transactions contemplated by the Seller Ancillary Documents based on arrangements made by or on behalf of the Seller.**

Often a prospective seller will engage an investment banker or some other type of broker to help it market the target company for sale to one or more prospective buyers, negotiate the purchase price, and otherwise manage the sale process. The fees that an investment banker charges a seller for these services differ from transaction to transaction, but are usually substantial in amount and tied to a percentage of the purchase price received by the seller for the target company. This representation and warranty gives the buyer comfort that all investment banker fees and similar fees will be borne solely by the seller. Sometimes a seller will cause the target company to engage an investment banker directly, instead of the seller engaging the investment banker directly, which could lead to the buyer being indirectly responsible for the investment banker fees (by virtue of owning the target company) if they are not paid at or prior to closing (see Section 4.24 regarding company brokers). As a result, buyers will often require (as part of Article II) that all brokers' fees be paid at the closing out of the purchase price proceeds.

> **Section 3.06 Amounts Owed to Seller. The Company does not owe and not otherwise obligated to pay the Seller any amount.**

This is a representation and warranty that the target company does not owe, and is not otherwise obligated, to pay the seller any amount. There are many ways in which a target company can become obligated to make payments to a stockholder of the company. It is not uncommon for a stockholder to loan money to its company or otherwise enter into a commercial transaction with its company, which obligates the company to make payments to the stockholder. The company may declare a dividend on its outstanding shares of common stock; however, the payment of that dividend often occurs on a date subsequent to the declaration. Accordingly, the dividend payment becomes an obligation owed to the company's stockholders. Thus, this representation and warranty simply confirms that there is a clean break between the seller and the company, and that the buyer will not have any obligation after the closing to pay seller more money by virtue of a commercial relationship between the seller and the company which will then be owned by the buyer. You will notice that this representation and warranty, and the related concept, ties into Section 4.21 of the Agreement regarding contracts between the company and its affiliates, which will be address later in this book.

ARTICLE IV
COMPANY REPRESENTATIONS & WARRANTIES

Author's Note: No contribution by the company. The Company will not have any liability to any Indemnifying Party as a result of any misrepresentation or breach of any representation or warranty contained in this Agreement or any certificate, schedule, instrument, agreement or other writing delivered by or on behalf of, or in respect of, the Company pursuant to this Agreement, any additional agreement or in connection with the transactions contemplated in this Agreement, or the breach of any covenant or agreement of the Company contained in this Agreement, any additional agreement or any certificate, schedule, instrument, agreement or other writing by or on behalf of, or in respect of, the Company pursuant to the terms of this Agreement, any additional agreement or in connection with the transactions contemplated by this Agreement. After the Closing, no Indemnifying Party will have any right to indemnification or contribution against the Company on account of any event or condition occurring or existing on or before the Closing Date.

Article IV sets forth the representations and warranties of the seller as to the business and operations of the target company. Occasionally a seller will try to argue that the company should be joined as a party to the document for the purpose of making the Article IV reps because the seller does not have sufficient knowledge of the company's day-to-day operations. This argument should be strongly resisted by the buyer and its counsel because it muddies the water as to whom between the company and the stockholders should be responsible for any breach of a company representation or warranty. It also confuses the true issue of which of the actual parties to the transaction (the buyer and the seller) should ultimately bear the risk of a representation or warranty being untrue or inaccurate. If the company is a party to the agreement for any purpose (such as pre-closing covenants in a transaction where there is a delay between signing and closing), then buyer's counsel should consider adding a disclaimer relieving the company from liability under the agreement to the extent that liability arises after the closing occurs. A sample of such a provision is set out in the Author's Note above and should be included, if appropriate, in the limits of liability set forth in Article VIII. As you may suspect, this is particularly important in a stock deal because the buyer acquires all liabilities of the target company.

Another issue that often comes up at this point where there is more than one seller is whether the company representations will be given jointly or severally by the sellers for purposes of indemnification. When dealing with multiple sellers, they will typically want to give the representation and warranties severally so that any loss resulting from them being untrue or inaccurate will not be borne by the sellers disproportionately in relation to the amount of purchase price the sellers receive. The buyer, on the other hand, will argue that it should not be the buyer's obligation to chase down all of the sellers and join them in a single action to obtain recovery for the full amount of losses resulting from a breach of a representation and warranty. Buyers will also argue that the sellers among themselves, not the buyer, should bear the credit risk of non-payment by their fellow sellers and resolve the disproportionality issue among themselves by entering into arrangement, such as a contribution agreement, among the sellers so that each seller agrees to contribute cash to cover his or her share of any loss that results from a breach or inaccuracy of any company representation or warranty. If the buyer, however, ultimately agrees that does eventually capitulate, the better solution is that the reps and indemnification should still be joint and several (so the buyer does not have to crack the nut of tracing responsibility for breach) but the disproportionality issue should be addressed in the limits of liability in Article VIII.

Lastly, the company representations and warranties in Article IV are a good starting place, but must be tailored to match the nature of the business being purchased and the specific findings in the buyer's due diligence investigation of the target company. For example, if the target company is a data analytics company, the representations and warranties around the intellectual property of the target company will need to be extremely strong since that is likely the most valuable asset of the target company. On the other hand, if the buyer is purchasing a waste collection and disposal company, it will probably be less concerned about the target company's intellectual property rights, and will likely be focused more on representations and warranties regarding compliance with environmental laws, possession of required permits and licenses, and compliance with labor laws. At the end of the day, the buyer's counsel needs to make sure that the company representations and warranties do the following: adequately cover the target company's key assets; address the primary risks inherent in the lines of business that the buyer will obtain; and adequately protect the buyer from any potential liabilities of the target company.

> **The Seller hereby [jointly and severally] represents and warrant to the Buyer as follows as of the Closing Date:**
>
> **Section 4.01 Organization and Good Standing. The Company is a corporation duly formed and validly existing under the Laws of the State of Delaware and has all requisite power and authority to own, lease and operate its properties and to carry on its business as now being conducted. The Company is duly qualified or registered as a foreign corporation to transact business under the Laws of each jurisdiction where the character of its activities or the location of the properties owned or leased by it requires such qualification or registration. The Seller has heretofore made available to the Buyer true, correct and complete copies of the Company's Organizational Documents as in effect on the Closing Date and the corporate record books with respect to actions taken by its stockholders and board of directors through the Closing Date. Schedule 4.01 contains a true, correct and complete list of the jurisdictions in which the Company is qualified or registered to do business as a foreign corporation.**

This is a fundamental representation and warranty that you should expect to find in almost every agreement for a commercial transaction. It ensures the buyer that the company is duly formed and validly existing under applicable law. This is particularly important given that the buyer will succeed to the corporate form of the company and will want to make sure that all corporate formalities have been observed so the buyer will continue to enjoy the limited liability protection afforded by the corporate veil. The representation and warranty also ensures that the buyer has been provided with true and accurate copies of the organization documents of the company and the minutes of board and stockholder meetings, which the buyer will need to maintain going forward after the closing.

> **Author's Note.** Buyer's tax counsel should compare the list of jurisdictions provided in Schedule 4.01 against the jurisdictions where the company files sales tax returns, and vice versa, for any consistencies.

> **Section 4.02 Authorization. The Company has the corporate power and authority to (a) execute and deliver each Company Ancillary Document, (b) perform its obligations under each Company Ancillary Document, and (c) consummate the transactions contemplated by each Company Ancillary Document. Each Company Ancillary Document has been duly executed and delivered by the Company, and constitutes the valid and binding agreement of the Company enforceable against the Company in accordance with its respective terms, subject to applicable bankruptcy, insolvency, reorganization, moratorium or other similar Laws affecting the enforcement of creditors' rights generally, general equitable principles and the discretion of courts in granting equitable remedies.**

Similar to the Organization and Good Standing representation and warranty in Section 4.01, this is a fundamental representation and warranty that you should expect to find in almost every agreement for a commercial transaction. It basically says the target company has the authority to undertake the transaction and to sign all the documents and perform all the obligations under the agreement that are required to close the transaction.

> **Section 4.03 Capital Stock. The authorized capital stock of the Company consists of [•] shares of common stock, par value $0.01 per share. All the issued and outstanding shares of capital stock of the Company (a) are duly authorized, validly issued, fully paid and nonassessable, (b) are held of record by the Seller, and (c) were not issued in violation of the preemptive rights of any Person or any agreement or Laws. Except as set forth on Schedule 4.03: (A) there are no outstanding options, warrants, rights, calls, commitments, conversion rights, rights of exchange, subscriptions, claims of any character, agreements, obligations, convertible or exchangeable securities or other plans or commitments, contingent or otherwise, relating to the capital stock or other equity interests of the Company, other than as contemplated by this Agreement; (B) there are no outstanding Contracts by which the Company is bound that grants any right to any stockholder of the Company or any other Person to purchase, redeem or otherwise acquire any outstanding shares of capital stock or other equity interests of the Company, or securities or obligations of any kind convertible into any shares of the capital stock or other equity interests of the Company; (C) there are no dividends which have accrued or been declared but are unpaid on the capital stock or other equity interests of the Company; (D) there are no outstanding or authorized stock appreciation, phantom stock, stock plans or similar rights with respect to the Company; and (E) there are no stockholder agreements, voting agreements or other similar agreements relating to the management of the Company by which a stockholder of the Company or the Company is bound. The Company has never purchased, redeemed or otherwise acquired any shares of its capital stock.**

The critical components of this representation and warranty is the accurate description of the capitalization of the target company. In particular, the seller is required to describe accurately all the equity securities of the target company that are outstanding and the owners of those securities. Accordingly, if post-closing a person not identified in this representation and warranty claims to be a holder of equity securities of the target company for whatever reason, then it would be a breach of this representation and warranty and the buyer would likely have a right to seek indemnification from the seller for such breach. Please note, if the target company has multiple classes of capital stock, stock options or other equity securities convertible into or exercisable for shares of capital stock, then this section will need to be substantially revised to reflect all the types of equity securities of the target company that are outstanding. A sample representation and warranty regarding a target company's outstanding stock options and the related stock option plan is set out below.

Sample Stock Option Representation and Warranty

The Company has reserved an aggregate of 2,500,000 shares of common stock for issuance pursuant to the Option Plan (including shares issued upon exercise of Options and shares subject to outstanding Options). Schedule 4.3(b) indicates for each Option, (i) the name of the holder of such Option ("Optionholder"), (ii) the state of residence or jurisdiction of incorporation or organization of such holder, (iii) the exercise price per share, date of grant and expiration date for such Option, (iv) the number of shares covered by such Option, (v) the vesting schedule for such Option, (vi) the extent such Option will be vested as of the Closing Date, prior to giving effect to any acceleration in connection with the transactions contemplated by this Agreement, (vii) whether such Option is an incentive stock option or a non-statutory stock option, (viii) whether the exercisability of such Option shall be accelerated in any manner by any of the transactions contemplated by this Agreement (ix) if such Option is held by a Person who is not an employee of the Company, the relationship of such Person to the Company. True, correct and complete copies of the Option Plan, the standard agreement under the Option Plan, and each agreement for each Option that does not conform to the standard agreement under the Option Plan have been delivered or otherwise made

> ***available by the Company to Buyer. All Options have been issued and granted in compliance with Laws and the Option Plan, and all shares of Company stock that may be issued upon exercise of Options will be (upon issuance in accordance with their terms) duly authorized, validly issued in accordance with Laws, fully paid and nonassessable. No Option has been granted with an exercise price less than the fair market value of a share of Company common stock as determined by the Board of Directors of the Company on the date of grant. All of the Options outstanding as of the Closing Date will terminate and be of no further force or effect at the Closing, and neither of the Company nor the Buyer shall, thereafter, have any liability or obligation, including any obligation to issue any security pursuant thereto or to pay or provide any consideration with respect thereto.***

The representation and warranty in Section 4.03 goes on to state that the shares are not to be subject to any voting agreements, shareholder agreements, rights of first refusal, or similar contracts. If during the due diligence and disclosure process it becomes apparent that the shares are in fact subject to any of these agreements, then the buyer's counsel should require the seller and the target company to cause these agreements to be terminated, effective as of the closing, as a condition to the buyer's obligation to close the transaction. With a simultaneous signing and closing structure, this would require the seller to start the termination process before the purchase agreement is signed by the parties.

> **Section 4.04 Subsidiaries. The Company does not own, and has never owned (whether directly or indirectly), any capital stock or other equities, securities or interests in any corporation, limited liability company, partnership, trust or other business entity.**

Section 4.04 is a representation and warranty that the target company basically does not have any subsidiaries, is not a party to a joint venture, and does not otherwise have any investments in any companies or other business entities. If it becomes apparent during diligence that the target company does in fact have one or more subsidiaries, is a party to a joint venture or otherwise owns equity in another entity, then this representation and warranty would need to be revised so that these investments are disclosed as exceptions to this representation and warranty. Additionally, a buyer and its counsel should consider whether all the operational representations and warranties should also apply to the target company's subsidiaries, and not just the parent company, especially if the subsidiaries directly own material assets and/or directly operate the business. The seller and its seller counsel, on the other hand, will want to ensure that the representations and warranties apply only to entities that are "controlled" by the target company and not entities where the target company is only a minority owner or has limited decision-making power, such as in a joint venture. This is because the target company may not have sufficient access to the information necessary to ensure that the representations and warranties can be made with respect to these entities. Additionally, the target company may not have had sufficient influence over the day-to-day operations of these entities to ensure they were operated within the parameters of the representations and warranties.

As a deal mechanics note, a seller will often ask whether it will own after the closing the equity securities that the target company owned. The answer is simply "no." These securities are assets of the target company, will remain with the target company, unless transferred to the seller prior to closing, and will, accordingly, become indirectly owned by the buyer as of the closing. A buyer will often ask whether it will be able to consolidate the financial results of the affiliated entities with those of the target company under GAAP. Generally, if the entity is at least 80 percent owned by the target company, then the financial results of the affiliated entities will be able to consolidate with those of the target company. However, if the ownership interest is greater than 51 percent but less than 80 percent, then a buyer should seek accounting advice as to whether it can consolidate the financial results of the target company's affiliates with those of the target company. Generally, if the target company owns 50 percent or less of an affiliated entity, then that affiliated entity's financial results cannot be consolidated with those of the target company.

> **Section 4.05 Absence of Restrictions and Conflicts. The execution and delivery of this Agreement, the Seller Ancillary Documents and the Company Ancillary**

> **Documents, the consummation of the transactions contemplated hereby and thereby, and the fulfillment of and compliance with the terms and conditions hereof and thereof do not or shall not (as the case may be), with the passing of time or the giving of notice or both, (a) conflict with or violate the Company's Organizational Documents; (b) except as described on Schedule 4.05, conflict with, result in any breach of, constitute a default (or an event that, with notice or lapse of time or both, would become a default) under, require any approval, consent or authorization of any Person pursuant to, or give to others any rights of termination, acceleration or cancellation of, any Material Contract or any other Contract, permit, franchise, license or other instrument applicable to the Company, (iii) conflict with or violate any Order to which the Company is a party or by which the Company or any of its properties are bound, or (iv) conflict with or violate any Law applicable to the Company [, except, in each case, as would not result in a Material Adverse Effect]. No consent, approval, order or authorization of, or registration, declaration or filing with, any Governmental Entity is required with respect to the Company in connection with the execution and delivery of this Agreement, the Seller Ancillary Documents or the Company Ancillary Documents, or the consummation of the transactions contemplated hereby or thereby.**

The absence of restrictions representation and warranty set forth in Section 4.05 with respect to the target company is very similar to the absence of restrictions representation and warranty set forth in Section 3.02 with respect to the seller. This representation and warranty also falls into the category of a "fundamental" representation and warranty, which you should expect to find in nearly all agreements for commercial transactions. With a focus on external compliance, the representations and warranties in Section 4.05 can be thought of as the counterpart to those set forth in Section 4.02 (authorization), which focuses on internal compliance. As such, this representation and warranty states that the execution of the stock purchase agreement and consummation of the transaction contemplated by it will not violate any contractual or other obligation to which the target company is a party or violate any law applicable to it. If any meaningful contract to which the target company is a party has a provision that requires the target company to seek the consent of, or give notice to, the counterparty with respect to the transaction, then the disclosure schedule for Section 4.05 will need to cross-reference the disclosure schedule for Section 4.13(a), which disclosure schedule identifies with an asterisk all such meaningful contracts.

Counsel for the seller typically will try to negotiate materiality qualifiers into this representation and warranty (see bracketed language above) so that minor restrictions and conflicts relating to contracts, orders and laws will not result in a breach of the representation and warranty. Typically, a buyer's counsel will resist adding materiality qualifiers given that there is a high degree of subjectivity and ambiguity when interpreting what a materiality qualifier actually means in this context. An alternative to adding a general materiality qualifier is to quantify the materiality threshold with a specific dollar amount. Accordingly, if there is a basket or deductible with respect to seller's indemnification obligations to the buyer (See Article VII), then the buyer's counsel will likely argue that such basket or deductible essentially functions as a materiality qualifier and, therefore, "materiality" qualifiers should be removed from the representation and warranty. A buyer's counsel can use this same argument to resist a seller attempting to add materiality qualifiers to other representations and warranties.

Section 4.06 Real Property.

(a) Schedule 4.06(a) sets forth a true, correct and complete legal description of each parcel of real property owned by the Company (together with all fixtures and improvements thereon) (collectively, the "Company Owned Real Property"). The Company has (and will continue to have at the Closing) good and marketable title to each parcel of the Owned Real Property, free and clear of all Liens other than Permitted Liens. [Alternative: The Company does not own, and have never owned, any real property.]

The representation and warranty in Section 4.06(a) requires the seller to list all real property owned by the target company. This representation and warranty follows a pattern that you will see often in this purchase agreement in that it requires the seller to list and identify a certain class of assets, here owned real property, and then will go on to make statements regarding the condition of the particular asset.

If a target company does have significant owned real property, then the buyer's counsel will want to ensure that the target company (not the seller) has good title to this property, that the property is fit for its intended use and the property (and the target company's ownership thereof) complies with all applicable laws and ordinances. This will mean that, during the due diligence stage, the buyer will need to conduct title searches on the owned property, review all mortgages and conveyance documents related to the property, and engage a specialist to conduct Phase I and II environmental site assessments of the property, all in an effort to gain better understanding of the real property assets to negotiate property representations and warranties in the purchase agreement. If the real property purportedly owned by the target company is actually titled in a seller's name (which is not uncommon), the buyer's counsel must consult with the buyer to determine whether the buyer expected this real property to be an asset of the target company. If so, the title to that real property must be transferred from the seller to the target company in connection with the closing of the transaction. If the seller is a joint tenant or tenants in common with the target company in the owned real property, then the seller will need to deliver a quit claim deed at the closing.

> **(b) Schedule 4.06(b) sets forth the true, correct and complete street address of each parcel of real property of which the Company is the lessee (together with all fixtures and improvements thereon) (the "Company Leased Real Property" and, together with the Company Owned Real Property, the "Company Real Property").**

The representation and warranty in Section 4.06(b) requires the seller to list all real property that the target company leases. The buyer's counsel will want to cross check the disclosure schedule to Section 4.13(a) in order to ensure that it has received and reviewed all lease agreements for such property. A buyer will often require a seller to deliver consent and estoppel certificates executed by the target company's landlords, consenting to the transaction and certifying that all rent payments have been made to date and there are no subsisting breaches under the lease documents.

> **(c) The Company has a valid leasehold interest in the Company Leased Real Property.**
>
> **(d) No portion of the Company Real Property, or any building or improvement located thereon, violates any Law, including those Laws relating to zoning, building, land use, fire, air, sanitation and noise control. Except for the Permitted Liens, no Company Real Property is subject to (i) any Order or, to the Knowledge of the Seller, threatened or proposed Order, or (ii) any rights of way, building use restrictions, exceptions, variances, reservations or limitations of any nature whatsoever.**

This representation and warranty also states that the real estate owned and leased by the target company does not violate any law and is not subject to any order or restrictions. The seller's counsel often takes issue with the first point on the grounds of materiality, and seeks to except immaterial breaches—to which the same lines of argument set forth in Section 4.05 equally apply.

The portion of this representation and warranty regarding the existence of restrictions often elicits some negotiations as well. As anyone who owns a house will know, almost all parcels of land are subject to a laundry list of zoning restrictions, setbacks, and other covenants that may be imposed by the county, state, or the developer. A seller typically will argue that it cannot possibly list all the applicable restrictions. Accordingly, it will attempt to qualify this statement with knowledge or materiality. Another solution we have seen in a recent transaction is to add a qualifier along the following lines: "Other than those imposed by municipal zoning or conservation of historical buildings regulations which are set forth in publicly available documents." This seemed like a reasonable compromise given that these ordinances and zoning regulations are all publicly available.

(e) [To the best of Seller's Knowledge], [t]he improvements and fixtures on the Company Real Property are in good operating condition and in a state of good maintenance and repair, ordinary wear and tear excepted, are adequate and suitable for the purposes for which they are presently being used. There is no condemnation, expropriation or similar proceeding pending or, to the Knowledge of the Seller, threatened against any of the Company Real Property or any improvement thereon. The Company Real Property constitutes all of the real property utilized by the Acquired Companies in the operation of the Business.

The second and third sentence of this representation are straightforward and seldom negotiated. The seller's counsel, however, will often take issue with the first sentence as being subjective and attempt to add a knowledge qualifier (see brackets above). The position is understandable because reasonable parties could differ regarding the "suitability" of any given improvement or fixture for which it is being used. That said, a buyer typically will resist on the grounds that a court is capable of resolving this question of fact and if a loss has been sustained in excess of the basket or deductible, then it is material and the seller should indemnify the buyer for such loss.

Real Estate Drafting Tips by Leah L. Weinberg, Associate General Counsel, Rouse Properties, Inc.

An attorney's comments to the representations in the real estate section of a stock purchase agreement will depend greatly on whether the attorney represents the buyer or seller. Here are a few key differences:

<u>Seller's Counsel</u>

- In Section 4.06(a), a seller's attorney should never agree to the representation that the target company has "good and marketable title" to the real property, since "good" and "marketable" are difficult standards to both define and attain. The preferred approach is to represent that the target company has "fee simple title" to the real property. A prudent buyer would obtain title reports on all owned real property and therefore should get comfortable with this representation.

- As a general matter, the seller's attorney will want to limit representations to those items that cannot be determined by the buyer's due diligence. For example, sometimes buyers ask for a representation that all owned real property has access to a public right-of-way. Seller's attorney should push back on this request, since access can be determined by the buyer ordering a survey of the property.
- Always try to insert materiality and knowledge qualifiers into the representations. The ideal knowledge qualifier would read as follows: "To Seller's actual knowledge, with no duty of inquiry…."

Buyer's Counsel

- When dealing with leased real property, pay close attention to the assignment of the lease or change of control of the tenant entity that will result from the merger. A buyer's attorney should be extremely diligent in reviewing the assignment and subletting provisions in the lease documents. The consent of the landlord under the lease may be required for the contemplated transaction, and the buyer's attorney does not want its client to be in default on day one after the transaction. If landlord consent is required, then these consents should be a condition of closing. The attorney may even request a representation from the seller that the leases listed on the schedule do or do not require consent for the transaction.
- Even though the buyer may receive estoppel certificates from landlords under the target company's leases, buyer's counsel should request a representation from the seller that there are no present defaults under the leases or any conditions in existence that, with notice or the passage of time or both, would constitute a default under the leases.
- During due diligence, a buyer's attorney should keep in mind any requirements of the buyer's lender. If the buyer's lender is going to want fee mortgages or leasehold mortgages on the owned or leased property, respectively, then the buyer's attorney will have to make sure that the assets are financeable. In addition, in the case of leased real property, landlord consents to leasehold mortgages and landlord lien waivers should be conditions to closing.

Section 4.07 Title to Assets; Related Matters. The Company has good and marketable title to all of their respective tangible personal property [and assets], free and clear of all Liens except Permitted Liens. All equipment and other items of tangible personal property and assets of the Company (a) are in good operating condition and in a state of good maintenance and repair, ordinary wear and tear excepted, (b) are usable in the regular and Ordinary Course, and (c) conform to all applicable Laws. To the Knowledge of the Seller, there is no defect or problem with any of such equipment, tangible personal property or assets, other than ordinary wear and tear. No Person other than the Company owns any equipment or other tangible personal property or assets situated on the Company's premises, except for the leased items that are subject to personal property leases. During the past [__] years, The Company has not sold, transferred or disposed of any assets, other than sales of inventory in the Ordinary Course.

The title to assets representation and warranty begins with a statement that the company has good title to all of its assets and personal property free and clear of any liens. This is probably one of the most important representations and warranties a seller makes in an asset deal but is sometimes overlooked in a stock deal where the focus is…you guessed it…the ownership of the stock. While this focus on stock ownership is important, a company with no assets is in most cases a worthless shell. Consequently, a buyer's counsel should pay close attention to this representation and warranty in so far as it functions to guarantee the turn-key nature of the business at the closing (i.e., that the company has all the assets that the buyer will need to operate the business as it was conducted under the seller's ownership).

> **Author's Note**: Occasionally (but more often than you would expect), the disclosure of non-company assets can be taken to the point of comedy where sellers disclose as an exception to this representation all personal chattels of employees located on premises (umbrellas, personal framed photographs, trophies, bobble head dolls, etc.).

Critical to this is the statement that no one else owns any of the assets situated on the company's premises. The buyer is likely counting on all the hard assets, such as laptops, printers, desks, chairs, forklifts, dump trucks, drill presses, etc., inventoried during due diligence to be on premises the day of the closing. If the buyer is going to have to buy any additional assets that are not coming along in the deal to run the business in the ordinary course, then it will want to know this ahead of time so that it can price the transaction accordingly. Similarly, the buyer will also want to know if any of the assets are subject to equipment leases. Depending on the way in which the deal is priced (and the leases are structured), the buyer may treat the leases as debt and require them to be paid-in full and title transferred to the company at the closing.

The seller's counsel should be cognizant that the Title to Assets representation and warranty can be a "backdoor" to other representations and warranties in that the class of assets is not defined. Accordingly, in many cases, a seller might attempt to limit the application of this representation and warranty to only "personal property and fixed assets" under the argument that other assets (e.g., real estate, intellectual property, and material contracts) are covered in various other representations and warranties in the stock purchase agreement. Buyer's counsel (often beating the table) will push that this is an overarching and fundamental representation regarding the turn-key nature of the business and will simultaneously attempt to expand the representation and warranty and carve it out from any limitations on liability.

Perhaps the more hotly contested item is the "Sufficiency of Assets" representation and warranty, which is the most important representation and warranty in an asset purchase transaction, but is often found as an add-on to the title representation and warranty set forth above in a stock purchase transaction. A typical Sufficiency of Assets representation and warranty will provide something along these lines:

> ***The properties and assets of the Company taken in the aggregate will be sufficient for Buyer's post-Closing operation of the Business in the Ordinary Course. Following the Closing Date, the Company will be permitted to continue to exercise all of its rights with respect to such properties and assets to***

the same extent had the transactions contemplated by this Agreement not occurred and without the payment of any additional amounts or consideration.

A seller will often resist giving this representation and warranty because it forces it to represent to a state of facts that exist after the closing and, to some extent, are outside of its control.

Section 4.08 Financial Statements.

(a) Attached as Schedule 4.08(a) are true, correct and complete copies of (i) the audited balance sheets with respect to the Company as of [________ ___, 20__], [________ ___, 20__] and [________ ___, 20__], and the related audited statements of income, stockholder's equity and cash flows for the fiscal years then ended (collectively, the "Audited Financial Statements"), and (ii) the unaudited consolidated balance sheet with respect to the Company as of [________ ___, 20__] (the "Balance Sheet") and the related unaudited statement of income, stockholder's equity and cash flows with respect to the Company as of and for the [____]-month period ended [________ ___, 20__] (the "Unaudited Financial Statements" and together with the Audited Financial Statements and the Balance Sheet, the "Financial Statements").

The first sentence of Section 4.08 requires the seller to provide and make representations and warranties with respect to the target's audited financial statements for the last three years and the unaudited financial statements for the stub period (the last full accounting period since the date of the most recent audited financial statements). Some buyers will go further and require a five-year look back, i.e., a representation and warranty on the five most recent audited financial statements. The stub period balance sheet is defined and is used as a reference point for certain target company representations and warranties within the definitive agreement aimed at bridging the gap between the date of the last balance sheet and the closing date.

Author's Note: Financial Terms:

- Balance Sheet: A financial statement that provides a snapshot of the company's financial condition at a given point in time (not a period) as expressed in terms of assets, liabilities, and stockholders' equity.
- Statement of Income: A financial statement that covers the reporting of revenue and expenses over an accounting period and allows a reader to track the top line down to the bottom line, from gross revenue to net revenue.
- Statement of Stockholder's Equity: A periodic financial statement that sets forth the major components of stockholders equity including capital stock, paid in capital, retained earnings, treasury stock, and unrealized loss on long-term investments and foreign currency translation gains.
- Statement of Cash Flows: A periodic financial statement that sets forth the cash position of the company. The SOCF allows a reader to evaluate the short-term viability of the company and its ability to pay bills in the ordinary course of business.

The Financial Statements have been prepared from, and are in accordance with, the Company's books and records, which books and records accurately reflect the Company's assets and liabilities and are maintained in accordance with GAAP consistently applied throughout the periods indicated, and such books and records have been maintained on a basis consistent with the Company's past practices. The Company maintains adequate internal accounting controls sufficient to provide reasonable assurances regarding the reliability of financial reporting and the preparation of annual financial statements for external purposes in accordance with GAAP. Each balance sheet included in the Financial Statements (including the related notes and schedules) fairly presents the consolidated financial position of the

> **Company as of the date of such balance sheet, and each statement of income, stockholder's equity and cash flows included in the Financial Statements (including the related notes and schedules) fairly presents the consolidated results of operations and changes in cash flows, as the case may be, of the Company or for the periods set forth therein, in each case in accordance with GAAP consistently applied during the periods involved. The Company has not changed any of its accounting (or tax accounting) policies, practices or procedures during the past [__] years.**

The rest of the representations and warranties in Section 4.08 are aimed at ensuring the accuracy of the target's historical financial statements (i.e., that they have been prepared in accordance with GAAP and accurately reflect the financial condition of the company.) The accuracy of the buyer's valuation, whether derived from a discounted cash flows analysis, market comparables, or revenue/EBITDA multiples, is rooted in the accuracy of the target's historical financial performance as manifest in its financial statements. If the numbers set forth in the target's financial statements are inaccurate, then the buyer's valuation will be inaccurate and the buyer may over pay for the target's stock. Consequently, it is essential that the buyer have comfort that the target's historical financial statements are correct and have been prepared in accordance with generally accepted accounting principles (or fully understand where sellers have deviated therefrom).

> **(b) All accounts receivable reflected on the Balance Sheet that have not been collected (collectively, the "Receivables") represent valid obligations of the customers of the Company arising from bona fide transactions entered into in the Ordinary Course, are current and are collectible (net of any reserves set forth on the Balance Sheet) without resort to legal proceedings or collections agencies. The Company has not factored any of the Receivables. During the**

past [__] years, the Company has collected all accounts receivable in the Ordinary Course.

The accounts receivable are assets of the target company that are being assigned value and purchased in connection with the transaction. Unlike cash on hand, which can be easily verified by forensic accountants by reviewing bank statements, the accuracy of accounts receivable can be verified only by checking invoices and calling customers/clients to confirm that they are valid. As a result, the buyer typically requires this representation and warranty as additional security regarding its due diligence regarding the target company's accounts receivable. Further, in net working capital guidelines, the parties may agree that only accounts receivable that have been collected prior to the final calculation of net working capital will be included as a current asset for purposes of adjusting the purchase price.

> **Author's Note: Factoring of Receivables:** This refers to the practice where a company sells its receivables to a third party at a discount on face value to raise cash on hand.

Section 4.09 No Undisclosed Liabilities. The Company does not have any Liabilities (whether absolute, accrued, contingent or otherwise) that are not adequately reflected or provided for in the Balance Sheet, except Liabilities that have been incurred since the date of the Balance Sheet in the Ordinary Course, and that are not (singly or in the aggregate) material to the Company.

Section 4.09 is a "catch-all" representation and warranty that states that any liabilities that are required to be disclosed on the balance sheet are so reflected. Seller's counsel often will try to limit the representation to apply only to GAAP liabilities. This effectively would exclude from the representation and warranties liabilities that the target company's accountants view as improbable or difficult to quantify.

Section 4.10 Absence of Certain Changes.

(a) Since [_________ __, 20__] and except as set forth on Schedule 4.10(a), there has not been (i) any Material

Adverse Effect, (ii) any damage, destruction, loss or casualty to property or assets of the Company with a value in excess of $[•] in the aggregate, whether or not covered by insurance, or (iii) any action taken to declare any dividend, pay or set aside for payment any dividend or other distribution, or make any payment to any Company Affiliated Person, other than the payment of salaries in the Ordinary Course or the pre-payment of any indebtedness of the Company.

This representation and warranty is commonly used to bridge the gap between a certain date and the date of the closing. Commonly the starting place is the date of the last balance sheet or most recent audited financial statement of the target company. It basically states that during this period, the target company has operated in the ordinary course of business and certain events have not occurred. The buyer will try to extend the look-back period as far back in the past as possible, while the seller will try to limit the look-back period to the most recent unaudited monthly financial statements or the last balance sheet, which ever date is closer to the date of definitive agreement signing date, and qualify the specific events by materiality and knowledge qualifiers.

(b) Since [__________ __, 20__] and except as set forth on Schedule 4.10(b), the Company has:

(i) conduct its businesses in the Ordinary Course and not engage in any new line of business;

This subsection captures the overarching intent of the representation and warranty that the target company has operated in the ordinary course of business, consistent with past practice.

(ii) not disposed of or permitted to lapse any right to the use of any Patent, Trademark, trade name, service mark, license or copyright (including any of the Company

Intellectual Property), or disposed of or knowingly disclosed to any Person, any trade secret, formula, process, technology or know-how not heretofore a matter of public knowledge;

The representation and warranty in this subsection is aimed at ensuring that the target company has not sold any of its key intellectual property.

(iii) not (A) sold any material asset, other than finished goods and inventory sold in the Ordinary Course and obsolete or damaged assets disposed of in the Ordinary Course, (B) created, incurred or assumed any indebtedness secured by any of the Company's assets, (C) granted, created, incurred or suffered to exist any Lien on any of the Company's assets that did not exist on the date of this Agreement, other than Permitted Liens, (D) incurred any material Liability (absolute, accrued or contingent), except in the Ordinary Course, (E) written-off any guaranteed check, note or account receivable, except in the Ordinary Course, (F) write-down the value of any asset or investment on the Company's books or records, except for depreciation and amortization in the Ordinary Course, (G) canceled any debt or waived any material claim or right, or (H) made any legally binding commitment for any capital expenditure to be made on or following the Closing Date;

The intent of the representation and warranty in this subsection is to ensure that the target company has not transferred any material asset, incurred any indebtedness, or granted any liens or other encumbrances on its assets.

> **(iv) not increased in any manner the base compensation of, or entered into any new bonus or incentive agreement or arrangement with, any of its employees, officers, directors or consultants, except in the Ordinary Course;**

The representation and warranty in this subsection gives the buyer comfort that it has accurately accounted for all employment and labor costs and that the seller has not made any promises (which may or may not be in anticipation of the sale) for extra compensation to any officers, directors, consultants, etc., that are not otherwise represented in the sale documents and may become binding obligations to the buyer.

> **(v) not paid or agreed to pay any additional pension, retirement allowance or other employee benefit under any Company Benefit Plan to any of its employees or consultants, whether past or present, except in the Ordinary Course;**

The representation and warranty in this subsection confirms that no additional payments have been made under any of the target company's benefits plans.

> **(vi) not adopted, amended or terminated any Company Benefit Plan or increase the benefits provided under any Company Benefit Plan, or promised or committed to undertake any of the foregoing in the future;**

The representation and warranty in this subsection takes one step back from 4.10(a)(vi) and confirms that the target company has not amended any of its benefits plans.

> **(vii) not amended or terminated any existing Employment Agreement or entered into any new Employment Agreement;**

The representation and warranty in this subsection ensures that the target company has not materially changed any of its labor contracts and assures the buyer that its audit of the company's employment agreements remains accurate at the time of the sale.

> **(viii) not made any Tax elections that would affect the Company or the Buyer or change any method or classification of accounting or application of any principles under GAAP; and**

The representation and warranty in this subsection ensures that the target company has not made any changes in its tax or accounting procedures. This is important because any change can be a red flag of other potential issues, including future liabilities that could be inherited by the buyer.

> **(ix) not authorized, or committed or agreed to take, any of the actions described in clauses (ii) through (viii) of this Section 4.10(b).**

The representation and warranty in this subsection effectively broadens the application of the previous representations and warranties by stating that the target company has not indirectly accomplished any of the restricted activities or committed to take any of them in the future.

> **Section 4.11 Legal Proceedings. Except as set forth on Schedule 4.11:**
>
> **(a) there is no Action pending or, to the Knowledge of the Seller, threatened, either at Law or in equity, against or affecting the Company or any of its properties or assets;**

The representation and warranty in Section 4.11(a) is a disclosure representation and warranty, which requires the seller to schedule all pending and threatened litigation relating to the target company. The seller's counsel may attempt to limit this representation to litigation in which the target company, or an officer, employee, or agent in its capacity as such is a named party. If the seller takes this tact, the buyer should minimally ensure that both current and past officers, employees, and agents are covered, and add directors and equity holders to the list.

From a diligence perspective, buyer's counsel will want to carefully review all disclosed actions to ensure that there is no pending "bet the company" claim that could have a major impact on the profitability of, or otherwise adversely impact, the target company. The buyer should also consider whether it is appropriate to require the seller to agree to indemnify the buyer for any disclosed actions or alternatively seek a reduction in the purchase price, particularly if any pending action is highly likely to result in a future loss to the target company or otherwise adversely affect the value of the target company in the future.

(b) there is no Order issued, promulgated or entered with respect to the Company or any of its properties or assets, in either case, that could adversely affect the operation of the Business; and

The representation and warranty in Section 4.11(b) is another disclosure representation and warranty, which requires the seller to disclose any court or governmental orders that restrict or otherwise adversely affect the target company.

(c) there are no Actions of the type described in Section 4.11(a) to which the Company, the Seller (in its capacity as an equity owner) or any director, officer or employee of the Company, was a party that have been adjudicated, appealed, withdrawn, dismissed, settled or otherwise resolved during the past [___ (__)] years.

The representation and warranty in Section 4.11(c) is another disclosure representation and warranty, which requires the seller to disclose historical litigation for a certain period preceding the closing date. This gives the buyer an idea of the type of litigation in which the target company is involved on a day-to-day basis.

Section 4.12 Compliance with Law; Permits.

(a) The Company is, and has been at all times, in compliance with all applicable Laws in all material

> **respects, [and except where such failure to comply would not have a Material Adverse Effect]. The Company has not been charged with, or received written notice that it is under investigation with respect to, and, to the Knowledge of the Seller, is not otherwise now under investigation with respect to, a violation of any applicable Law.**

Corporations, like people, are required to comply with the complex web of city, county, state, and federal laws, regulations and ordinances that comprise the legal ecosystem of the jurisdiction in which they operate. Along those lines, this representation and warranty requires the seller to guarantee that the target company is, and has been, in compliance with applicable laws and is not subject to any actual or threatened government actions. It is a broad representation and warranty and, while qualified by materiality, covers all types of laws, regulations, and ordinances and stretches back from the closing date to the formation of the company. A seller's counsel can attack several of these points by either limiting the compliance with law look-back period to a set number of years or taking the more aggressive position of striking the historical compliance portion of the representation altogether. Another common point of attack by a seller is to attempt to qualify the representation and warranty by reference to material adverse effect as set forth above in brackets.

> **Author's Note:** You may have noticed that compliance with laws is covered in other representations in addition to this Section 4.12. For example 4.14(a) (Tax Laws); 4.06(d) (Real Estate Laws); 4.15(iv) (Benefits Laws); 4.16(viii) Labor Laws; and 4.18 (Environmental Laws). You may think this is redundant, and it is. But there is a good reason for this. The limits imposed on the seller's indemnification obligations often have exceptions for certain sections, which more often than not include the specific sections set forth above.

Conversely, the buyer's counsel can seek to expand the investigations portion of the representation and warranty by requiring the seller to represent that there exists "no state of facts, that after notice or lapse of time or both, reasonably could be expected to give rise to any such investigation of other governmental action."

(b) The Company has filed all reports required to be filed with any Governmental Entity and possesses each permit, license, franchise, approval, certificate, consent, waiver, concession, exemption, order, registration, notice, ruling, decision, determination or other authorization of any Governmental Entity necessary for it to own, lease and operate its assets and to carry on its business as currently conducted (each, a "Permit"). Schedule 4.12(b) sets forth a true, correct and complete list of the Permits. The Company is in compliance in all material respects with each Permit it possesses and no suspension or cancellation of any Permit is pending or, to the Knowledge of the Seller, threatened. The Company has not received any notice of any Action relating to the revocation or modification of any Permit, and none of the Permits will be subject to suspension, modification, revocation or nonrenewal as a result of the execution and delivery of this Agreement or the consummation of the Transactions.

The laws of certain jurisdictions require certain businesses to maintain specific permits to operate. The types of permits required, and the labor and expense of obtaining such permits, vary based on how heavily the applicable business is regulated. On one end of the spectrum, a simple relatively unregulated business like a software provider may need only a county business license, which can often be acquired online or with $25 and a trip to the court house. On the other end of the spectrum, more heavily regulated businesses such as airlines, require a multiphase federal permitting process, in-depth investigations, and hefty fees that can cost thousands of dollars.

The purpose of this representation and warranty is to ensure (1) that the target company has all licenses and permits that are required for it to operate its business in the ordinary course; (2) that the target company is in compliance with all its license and permit requirements, and (3) that none of its licenses or permits will be adversely affected by the transaction (i.e., do not require notice or consent of the issuing agency and do not otherwise cause the license or permit to become invalid or ineffective). Buyer's counsel should review each license and permit to ensure that it does not have any provision that could require the buyer to reapply for the license or permit as a result of the transaction or otherwise cause the license or permit to become ineffective or require notice to be given to the issuing agency as a result of the transaction. If any of these types of provisions are uncovered, the parties should consider whether it is appropriate to restructure the transaction with a delay between sign and closing and the inclusion of the consent of the issuing agency to the transaction as a condition to closing.

A seller's attorney often will try to dull the edge of this representation and warranty by adding materiality and knowledge qualifiers to limit the scope to only those licenses and permits that are most important from the seller's perspective.

Regulatory/Compliance Note by Robert W. Kamerschen, General Counsel & Corporate Secretary, Aaron's Inc.

- The scope and nature of regulatory/compliance due diligence review in connection with a particular transaction and the related representations and warranties in the purchase agreement will largely be determined by the specific industry in which the target company is engaged. The industry designation will usually determine the applicable state and/or federal regulator with enforcement powers. Analysis around how active the regulator has been in enforcing its authority against the particular industry will be an important due diligence determination.
- Notwithstanding the foregoing, regardless of industry, participation in the international marketplace (by virtue of employing foreign nationals, conducting transnational transactions or ownership of subsidiaries in other counties) will subject a target company to additional US regulatory compliance issues, including without limitation, the Foreign Corrupt Practices Act, the Export Administration Act and the Immigration and Nationality Act.
- Further, target companies located in foreign countries may be subject to additional compliance obligations under the laws of such jurisdiction.
- A purchaser must carefully examine this web of foreign and domestic legal compliance obligations to identify any potential pitfalls.
- Such analysis should minimally include the following questions: (1) does the target company have a dedicated compliance program? (2) has the target company had any compliance issues or been the subject of

any governmental investigations in the past? (3) does the target company have business relationships with the government or any state owned entities? (4) does the target entity conduct business in any jurisdictions which are known to have corruption issues?

Section 4.13 Material Contracts.

(a) Schedule 4.13 sets forth a true, correct and complete list of all material Contracts to which the Company is a party or by which any of its assets or properties is bound (each, a "Material Contract" and collectively, the "Material Contracts") (other than the Employment Agreements reset forth on Schedule 4.15, the Company Benefit Plans set forth on Schedule 4.16(a) and insurance policies on Schedule 4.18), including without limitation:

The contractual arrangement to which a company is a party provides a blueprint of the economic relationships between the company and its customers, suppliers, partners, lenders, landlords, governmental entities, and other players in its business environment. A buyer can learn a great deal about a company through a forensic analysis of its contracting practices and review of its contracts. The representation and warranty above requires the seller to identify all material contracts to which the target company is a party or by which any of its assets or properties are bound. It then continues on to provide the non-inclusive list of types of contracts set out below. This is generally one of the most time-intensive disclosure schedules for the seller to prepare.

(i) all bonds, debentures, notes, loans, credit or loan agreements or loan commitments, mortgages, indentures, guarantees or other Contracts relating to the borrowing of money or binding upon any properties or assets (real, personal or mixed, tangible or intangible);

This subsection describes all of the target company's debt documents. If any of these types of agreements are disclosed, the buyer will need to consider whether all debt represented by these agreements should be paid off at closing from the purchase price proceeds and payoff letters from the creditors delivered as a closing condition. This is based on the fact that many purchase price valuations are based on the assumption that the target company is free of debt.

> **(ii) all leases relating to the Company Real Property or other leases or licenses involving any properties or assets (whether real, personal or mixed, tangible or intangible) involving an annual commitment or payment of more than $[•] individually by the Company;**

This subsection describes all real estate leases held by the target company and ties into the seller's representation and warranty regarding real estate set forth in Section 4.06. Please see note on materiality qualifiers set out above.

> **(iii) all Contracts that limit or restrict the Company or any of its Affiliates or any of its officers or key employees from engaging in any business in any jurisdiction;**

This subsection covers all non-competition agreements applicable to the target company, its officers or employees. A buyer should carefully examine the scope and term of any non-competition agreement to determine if it will affect the buyer's ability to own and operate the target company post-closing. For example, the buyer may have synergy value in the purchase price valuation that assumes the ability to sell the target company's products and/or services through the buyer's existing operations in a given locality. If a non-competition agreement covers this territory, it may impair the buyer's ability to obtain the projected revenue and therefore result in buyer overpaying for the target company. Moreover, the scope of a non-competition agreement might extend to the affiliates of the restricted entity. If this is the case, a buyer might actually restrict its own operations and fall under the non-competition agreement by virtue of becoming affiliated with the restricted target company.

(iv) all Contracts for capital expenditures or the acquisition or construction of fixed assets, which require the Company to pay more than $[•];

This subsection requires disclosure of all CAPEX and contracts regarding the acquisition of assets that require a cash commitment by the target company in excess of a certain mutually agreed threshold. Please see the discussion above in the Author's Note regarding materiality in contracts disclosures.

(v) all Contracts that grant any Person an increased payment or benefit, or accelerated vesting, upon the execution of this Agreement or the Closing or in connection with the Transactions;

This subsection requires disclosure of all contracts relating to "triggered contingencies" that arise from the consummation of the sale of stock contemplated by the stock purchase agreement. This includes relicensing fees, acceleration clauses and, to the extent not covered in the employment agreements disclosed on Schedule 4.15, parachute payments, phantom stock triggering events and other transaction bonuses. Triggered contingencies are often treated in a similar manner to closing date indebtedness and paid at the closing out of the purchase price proceeds.

(vi) all Contracts granting any Person a Lien on all or any part of any material asset of the Company;

This subsection covers all agreements granting security interests in any of the target company's assets. A buyer should cross-check disclosures against this representation and warranty against the publicly filed lien search results conducted during diligence.

(vii) all Contracts for the cleanup, abatement or other actions in connection with any Hazardous Materials, the remediation of any existing environmental condition or relating to the performance of any environmental audit or study;

This subsection covers any agreements relating to environmental conditions or hazardous waste. A buyer should take very seriously any disclosures against this representation, as environmental remediation can be an extremely expensive and time-involved endeavor, which could disrupt the normal course operation of the business. We have seen situations where the cost of environmental remediation was actually greater that the purchase price for the target company.

> **(viii) all Contracts granting to any Person an option or a first refusal, first-offer or similar preferential right to purchase or acquire any asset of the Company;**

This subsection refers to contracts granting preferential rights to third parties with respect to the purchase of the assets of the target company. These are basically restraints on the target company's ability to freely transfer and deal with its assets. The difference between a right of first refusal and a right of first offer is explored in the Author's Note.

> **Author's Note: ROFR v. ROFO.** A right of first refusal and a right of first offer are both contractual provisions that require a company to offer to sell the subject asset to the beneficiary of such right prior to transferring it to any third party. The difference between these two clauses is essentially one of timing. A right of first offer requires the company to offer the subject asset to the beneficiary prior to offering to sell it to any third party. A right of first refusal is triggered later in the sale process. Once a deal in principle regarding the asset has been finalized with a third party, the company must offer to sell to the beneficiary of the right, who can elect to step into the shoes of the potential purchaser and acquire the asset on the terms agreed to with the other potential purchaserrms.

> **(ix) all Contracts with any agent, distributor or representative that are not terminable without penalty on advance notice of fewer than thirty (30) days;**

This subsection requires the seller to disclose all distribution agreements that cannot be terminated on with advance notice of fewer than thirty days.

(x) all Contracts for the granting or receiving of a license, sublicense or franchise or under which any Person is obligated to pay or has the right to receive a royalty, license fee, franchise fee or similar payment;

This subsection requires the disclosure of all inbound and outbound license and franchise agreements and any other royalty agreements.

(xi) all Contracts (A) with respect to Company-Owned Intellectual Property licensed or transferred to any third party (other than end-user licenses in the Ordinary Course), or (B) pursuant to which a third party has licensed or transferred any Company Intellectual Property to the Company;

This subsection requires the disclosure of all inbound and outbound contracts regarding the target company's intellectual property. The buyer should cross-check this schedule against the disclosures the seller makes regarding company intellectual property in response to Section 4.18.

(xii) all Contracts providing for the indemnification or holding harmless of any officer, director or employee of the Company or other Person;

This subsection requires the disclosure of all contracts pursuant to which the target company has agreed to indemnify or hold harmless any other person. It is not uncommon for a company to agree to indemnify, hold harmless, and defend their employees, officers, and business partners for certain claims incurred in the ordinary course of business. Often times, a seller will attempt to limit this representation and warranty to only those indemnity obligations that flow to officers, employees, and directors of the target company.

(xiii) all Contracts involving (A) the sale or purchase of assets or capital stock (or other

equity interests) of any Person (other than inventory in the Ordinary Course), or (B) a merger, consolidation, business combination or similar extraordinary transaction;

This subsection requires the disclosure of all divestiture and acquisitions contracts to which the target company is a party. It is important for a buyer to review these contracts in detail as they will likely provide for substantial rights and obligations of the target company. If the target company is the seller in a particular transaction, the buyer's counsel will need to review the indemnities and limits of liabilities set forth in the agreements and counsel the buyer of potential future exposure to third parties under the agreement. If, conversely, the target company is the purchaser in the subject transaction, the buyer will need to focus on the disclosure schedules to the agreement to determine the known liabilities and the scope of the target company's rights to indemnification and any limits of liability under the agreement. It should be noted that sellers are often reluctant to disclose these agreements because a buyer can use the terms as precedent in the negotiation of the current stock purchase agreement.

(xiv) all joint venture or partnership Contracts and all other Contracts providing for the sharing of any profits;

Joint ventures are alliances between two or more parties for a particular business purpose and can be structured as a joint ownership of a business entity (e.g., ownership in a common limited liability company or limited partnership) or a contractual relationship (joint marketing/co-marketing relationships or strategic alliances). This subsection requires disclosure of all agreements to which the target company is a party regarding these joint venture relationships. While the type of agreements vary based on the underlying structure of the joint venture, they all typically have governance terms (describing how the joint venture will make decisions and operate), profit sharing/royalty terms (describing how payments will be calculated and distributed), provisions restricting transfer or assignment of the parties' interest in the joint venture (ROFRs and ROFOs as discussed above) and termination provisions. Joint venture agreements also commonly have non-competition covenants to ensure that the joint venture partners are not competing with the efforts of the joint venture. Any time a joint venture involves two large or dominant players in a particular market, the buyer's counsel should conduct an analysis to ensure that such arrangements are compliant with antitrust laws.

> ***all supplier Contracts (excluding purchase orders individually requiring payments by the Company of an amount less than $[●] per year) for the provision of goods or services to the Company;***

If the target company's business depends on the inputs of goods or services from third parties for the production and delivery of its products and services to target company customer and end-users, it will be critical for a buyer to understand the target company's relationship with these suppliers. Not all supply relationships are contracted, some are carried out on an *ad hoc* basis by way of purchase orders. At the other end of the spectrum are long-term requirements supply agreements that require the target company to purchase all of its requirements for a certain good or service from a certain supplier. As consideration for such a commitment, the supplier will usually agree to provide such good or service exclusively to the target company conditioned upon the achievement of certain purchasing milestones.

With any contracted supply arrangement, it is important for the buyer to understand the termination and pricing provisions. In many cases, a buyer will include cost-savings synergies in its purchase price model due to of post-closing economies of scale or vertical integration. These synergies are premised on the assumption that the target company will be able to favorably alter its post-closing supply relationships. Such calculations will need to be adjusted to account for any long-term supply agreements at unfavorable pricing that cannot be terminated upon short notice and without penalty.

On the contrary, if the target company's business model is dependent on the provision of a particular input that is not readily available from other suppliers, the buyer will need to assess the risk of the supplier terminating the agreement. In this case, the buyer's counsel will need to pay close attention to the termination and change of control provisions set forth in the relevant supply agreement. The buyer may also wish to conduct telephone or in-person meetings with these "linchpin" suppliers to obtain additional comfort that the relationship will continue post-closing.

Any time a supply agreement provides for exclusivity or price fixing among large or dominant market participants, buyer's counsel should conduct an analysis to ensure compliance with antitrust laws.

(xv) all customer Contracts for the provision of goods or services by the Company;

While supply agreements speak to the terms and conditions surrounding the inputs of the business, the customer contracts paint the picture of the target company's outputs. Each company documents its relationship with its customers in different ways. Like the supply arrangements discussed above, these can be papered by purchase order on a "one-off" basis, term sheet/pricing schedules or, with respect to more long-term relationships, with formal agreements that provide for material terms such as exclusivity, pricing, intellectual property rights, term/termination, and indemnification.

From a business perspective, the most important terms of the customer contracts are often pricing, term, and termination. If a substantial portion of a target company's revenue is contracted under long-term contracts, the buyer can project the target company's future earning with greater certainty. This is important where the buyer is using a discounted cash flows valuation method that establishes the purchase price based on the net present value of the projected returns. However, if a target company's contracts can be terminated at the customers' convenience or because of the consummation of the transaction pursuant to a change of control provision, then this certainty is decreased.

As discussed in the context of "linchpin" suppliers above, if a substantial portion of the target company's revenue is generated by a small group of customers, the buyer may wish to meet with each of these significant customers to further diligence the relationships and obtain more comfort that these customers will not terminate or seek to diminish its relationship with the target company post-closing as a result of the transaction.

It is also important for a buyer to understand pricing arrangements and any contractual limitations on the buyer's ability to set prices post-closing. As noted above, any price floors among substantial market players should be analyzed for antitrust compliance. Customer contracts should also be reviewed for "most favored nations" pricing clauses that require that the price a particular client is charged by the target company be as good or better than the prices offered to the target company's other customers.

(xvi) all outstanding powers of attorney empowering any Person to act on behalf of the Company; and

This subsection requires disclosure of all powers of attorney that grant any person the ability to act on behalf of the target company. A buyer may want to have some of these powers of attorney terminated as a condition to closing and new powers of attorney emplaced empowering buyer's designees. Of particular importance are powers of attorney related to the banking and financial affairs of the target company and those related to making filings with governmental agencies such as the IRS.

(xvii) all existing Contracts and commitments (other than those described in subsections (i) through (xvi) of this Section 4.13(a)) (A) involving an annual commitment or annual payment to or from the Company of more than $[•] individually or (ii) that is material to the Company or the Business.

This subsection is a "catch-all" provision intended to capture all material contracts, as denominated by reference to a dollar-based materiality qualifier, that are not otherwise covered by the specific classes of contracts set forth above.

(b) The Seller has made available to the Buyer true, correct and complete copies of all Material Contracts. Each Material Contract is legal, valid, binding and enforceable in accordance with its terms with respect to the Company and each other party to such Material Contract. There is no existing material default or breach by the Company under

> **any Material Contract (or event or condition that, with notice or lapse of time or both could constitute a material default or breach), and there is no such material default (or event or condition that, with notice or lapse of time or both, could constitute a material default or breach) with respect to any third party to any Material Contract. Except as set forth on Schedule 4.13(b), the Company is not participating in any discussions or negotiations regarding modification of, or amendment to, any Material Contract or entry in any new Contract that would constitute a Material Contract. <u>Schedule 4.13(a) identifies with an asterisk each Material Contract set forth therein that requires the consent of, or notice to, the other party thereto to avoid any breach, default or violation of such Contract in connection with the Transactions.</u>**

Here, the seller is representing and warranting that (1) it has provided the buyer with copies of all the material contracts, (2) all such agreements are legally binding on the target company and the counterparties thereto, and (3) neither the target company nor any contracting parties are in breach of such agreements. The seller's counsel should be cautious in agreeing to represent or warranty to the binding nature or absence of breach of agreements with respect to any third parties. Many sellers will attempt to soften this representation and warranty by the addition of a knowledge qualifier.

The last sentence in Section 4.13(b) (underlined above) requires the seller to identify all material contracts that contain change of control provisions or otherwise require notice and/or consent in connection with the transaction. As discussed above in the commentary to Sections 4.13(a)(xv) and (xvi), it is crucial for the buyer to identify any agreements that require consent in connection with the transaction so a determination can be made whether such consent should be obtained as a condition to closing, or in the alternative, the buyer is willing to run the risk of breach of that contract which might enable the counterparty to terminate the contract. It should be noted, that while change of control provisions arguably have the greatest potential economic impact on the target company when found in customer and supplier contracts, they are commonly found in lease agreements, debt documents, software licenses, and many other types of agreements.

Author's Note: Anti-Assignment Clauses versus Change of Control Provisions. There is often some confusion regarding the difference between an "anti-assignment clause" and a change of control provision. The former will generally state that the subject agreement cannot be transferred or assigned without the prior written consent of the counterparty. This requirement would be triggered when a transaction is structured as an asset deal, because the contracts, together with all other assets of the seller, are being transferred to the buyer. However, these provisions are not triggered in a stock deal because the stock, rather than the contracts, are being transferred (i.e., the contracting parties are the same before and after the closing).

Section 4.14 Tax Returns; Taxes.

(a) All Tax Returns required to have been filed by or with respect to the Company under applicable Laws have been timely filed, and each such Tax Return was correct and complete in all material respects and was prepared in substantial compliance with all applicable Laws. All Taxes due and owing by or with respect to the Company (whether or not shown as due on any Tax Return) have been paid. The Company is not the beneficiary of any extension of time within which to file any Tax Return. No claim has ever been made or, to the Knowledge of the Seller, threatened by a Governmental Entity in a jurisdiction where the Company does not file Tax Returns that the Company is or may be subject to taxation by that jurisdiction.

The intent of the representation and warranty in Section 4.14(a) is to ensure that the buyer will not have any liability for taxes arising from the seller's ownership or operation of the target company prior to the closing. More specifically, the representation and warranty states that (1) the target company has filed tax returns in all jurisdictions where it is required to do so, (2) the target company has paid all taxes when due, (3) none of the target company's tax returns remain open pursuant to an extension, and (4) no taxing authority has claimed the target company needs to file tax returns in any jurisdictions where it does not file returns. As a general note, given the magnitude of potential tax claims, it is always advisable for the buyer to engage tax advisors to perform due diligence on the target company's tax compliance.

> **(b) The Company has not received from any Governmental Entity (including in jurisdictions where the Company has not filed any Tax Return) any (i) written or, to the Knowledge of the Seller, oral notice indicating an intent to open an audit or other review, (ii) request for information related to Tax matters, or (iii) notice of deficiency or proposed adjustment for any amount of Tax proposed, asserted, or assessed by any Governmental Entity against the Company. Schedule 4.14(b) lists all federal, state, local and foreign income and sales and use Tax Returns filed with respect to the Company for taxable periods ended on or after [________ __, 20__], indicates which of such Tax Returns have been audited, and indicates which of such Tax Returns currently are the subject of audit. The Seller has delivered or otherwise made available to the Buyer true, correct and complete copies of all federal income Tax Returns that include the income of the Company, examination reports that may affect the Tax liability attributable to the Company, and statements of deficiencies assessed against or agreed to by the Company for taxable periods beginning on or after [________ __, 20__].**

The first sentence of Section 4.14(b) targets the relationship between the target company and the taxing authorities and the absence of any correspondence with such taxing authorities regarding any actual or potential audit, review or tax deficiency. The second sentence of Section 4.14(b) requires the seller to identity all tax returns that the target company has filed for a period of time prior to closing, and indicate whether such returns have been audited. That last sentence is a representation that the buyer has been provided with true and accurate copies of all federal income tax returns, together with any related documentation and correspondence with any tax examiner or taxing authority.

> **(c) There are no Liens for Taxes (other than Taxes not yet due and payable) upon any of the Company's assets.**
>
> **(d) The Company has withheld and paid all Taxes required to have been withheld and paid in connection with amounts paid or owing to any employee, independent contractor, creditor, stockholder, or other third party.**

Tax laws require corporations to withhold and pay taxes on behalf of certain third persons. Subsection 4.14(d) contains a representation that the target company has in fact made such withholdings and remitted them to the appropriate taxing authority. This representation most often comes into play and provides a buyer protection in the event that the target company fails to withhold taxes with respect to employees that are miss-categorized as contractors.

> **(e) The Company has not waived any statute of limitations in respect of Taxes or agreed to any extension of time with respect to a Tax assessment or deficiency.**

Buyers often make risk calculations and conduct due diligence based on the statute of limitations of an underlying claim. However, it is possible in certain circumstances for a taxpayer to waive the application of the statute of limitations. If the buyer is not aware that such a waiver has been granted, its risk calculation will be inaccurate and due diligence will be insufficient in scope.

> **(f) The Company is not a party to any Contract or other arrangement that has resulted or would result, separately or in the aggregate, in the payment of any "excess parachute payment" within the meaning of**

Section 280G of the Code (or any corresponding provision of state, local or foreign Tax Law).

A "parachute payment" or a "golden parachute" is a reference to compensatory payment made to executives, officers or other employees of the target company because of the "change of control" with the transaction. These can take many forms, including, but not limited to, stock options, restricted stock, phantom stock, cash retention bonuses, and cash transaction bonuses. While a full discussion of Section 280G of the Internal Revenue Code is beyond the scope of this book, a buyer and its counsel should be aware that, among other things, parachute payments in excess of certain thresholds trigger tax penalties to the recipient, are not tax deductible to the corporation and require certain special corporate approvals. Consequently, buyer's or seller's counsel should promptly consult with tax advisors if they believe that a parachute payment may be triggered in connection with the transaction.

Section 4.15 Company Benefit Plans.

(a) Schedule 4.15(a) contains a true, correct and complete list of the Company Benefit Plans and any special tax status enjoyed by such Company Benefit Plan is noted on Schedule 4.15(a).

Section 4.15(a) requires the buyer to list all benefit plans maintained by the target company and indicate whether these plans are subject to any special tax status. "Company benefit plans" include, without limitation, incentive compensation plans, pensions and other retirement plans, equity compensation plans and health, medical, dental, and legal benefits plans (a full list of coverage can be found in the definitions).

(b) Except as set forth on Schedule 4.15(b):

(i) The Company's records accurately reflect the employment or service histories of each of their respective employees, independent contractors, contingent workers and leased employees, including their hours of service, and all such records are maintained in a usable form.

Federal and state labor and employment laws, such as the Fair Labor Standards Act require employers to maintain true and accurate records of employees' and contractors' service histories. A purchaser's due diligence investigation will typically involve a review of 3 to 5 years of employment records for purposes of accessing historical risk arising from labor and employment practices. Any due diligence investigation will place special emphasis on human resources files including employee complaints and subsequent investigations.

> **(ii) No Company Benefit Plan or ERISA Affiliate Plan is or was subject to Title IV of ERISA or Section 412 of the Code, and no Company Benefit Plan or ERISA Affiliate Plan is or was a "multiemployer pension plan" (as defined in Section 3(37) of ERISA) or subject to Section 302 of ERISA. The Company has not terminated or withdrawn from or sought a funding waiver with respect to, and no fact exists that could reasonably be expected to result in a termination or withdrawal from or seeking a funding waiver with respect to, the Company Benefit Plan that is subject to Title IV of ERISA. The Company has not incurred, and no fact exists that reasonably could be expected to result in, liability to the Company as a result of a termination, withdrawal or funding waiver with respect to an ERISA Affiliate Plan.**

"ERISA" is the Employee Retirement Income Security Act of 1974. It is a federal law that regulates the tax treatment of pension and other employee benefit plans and related transactions. The representation above assures the buyer that the company's benefit plans have not experienced an event that could lead to ERISA regulatory intervention and/or plan liability under the statute (i.e., that the target company's benefits plans are essentially "healthy" under ERISA).

ERISA is a complex regulatory scheme which is outside the scope of this book. Any purchase that involves significant employee benefits or pension plans should involve an ERISA specialist.

> **(iii) No Company Benefit Plan or ERISA Affiliate Plan is or was a "multiple employer welfare arrangement" (as defined in Section 3(40) of ERISA).**

A "multiple employer welfare arrangement" (MEWA) is an arrangement or plan that provides health and/or other welfare benefits to employees of two or more unrelated employers. The purpose of MEWAs is to allow small employers to pool resources under a single plan to achieve economies of scale. A purchaser should note that the Federal pre-emption of ERISA does not apply to MEWAs and thus they are subject to burdensome multistate regulatory compliance.

> **(iv) Each Company Benefit Plan has been established, registered, qualified, invested, operated and administered in all respects in accordance with its terms and in compliance with ERISA, the Code and all Applicable Benefit Laws. The Company has not incurred, and no fact exists that reasonably could be expected to result in any liability to the Company with respect to any Company Benefit Plan or any ERISA Affiliate Plan, including any liability, tax, penalty or fee under ERISA, the Code or any Applicable Benefit Law (other than to pay premiums, contributions or benefits in the Ordinary Course).**

This representation is a general assertion that the Company Benefit Plans are in compliance with ERISA and applicable laws.

> **(v) No fact or circumstance exists that could adversely affect the tax-exempt status of a Company Benefit Plan that is intended to be tax-exempt. Further, each Company Benefit Plan intended to be "qualified" within the meaning of Section 401(a) of the Code and the trusts maintained thereunder**

that are intended to be exempt from taxation under Section 501(a) of the Code has received a favorable determination or other letter indicating that it is so qualified based on the terms of the plan or plans as currently in effect, and all amendments required to be adopted on or before the date of this Agreement have been timely and properly adopted.

The tax-exempt nature of a Company Benefit Plan is one of the most essential aspects of such a plan, and any event or plan mismanagement that could impact this exempt status creates a significant risk of future exposure. The loss of tax-exempt status for a plan that is intended to be qualified with the meaning of ERISA will inevitably require significant effort and resources to return to compliant status.

(vi) No insurance policy or any other Contract affecting any Company Benefit Plan requires or permits a retroactive increase in premiums or payments due thereunder. The level of insurance reserves under each insured Company Benefit Plan is reasonable and sufficient to provide for all incurred but unreported claims.

This provision is a desirable representation to the buyer in that it guarantees a level of predictability with regard to plan-related budgeting. Essentially, the seller is warranting that there are no known circumstances that will result in a "surprise" increase in premiums, and that the reserve cash under the plan is sufficient to cover any expected claims.

(vii) The execution and delivery of this Agreement and the consummation of the Transactions will not (A) entitle any current or former employee, director, officer, consultant, independent contractors, contingent worker or leased employee (or any of their dependents, spouses or beneficiaries) of the

Company to severance pay, unemployment compensation or any other payment, or (B) accelerate the time of payment or vesting, or increase the amount of compensation due any such individual.

This representation is an assurance by sellers that the purchase and sale transactions contemplated by the Agreement will not trigger any requirement that the target company pay severance or other employment-related payment obligations to any person. Any disclosed "triggered contingencies" will generally be paid by or on behalf of the Company from the purchase price at the Closing.

(viii) No Company Benefit Plan provides for post-retirement medical or other welfare benefits other than the medical benefits required to be provided under Part 6 of Subtitle B of Title I of ERISA.

Typically most employers do not provide for post-retirement benefits in excess of that required by ERISA. The purpose of this representation is to ensure that any such benefits maintained by the target company are duly disclosed.

(ix) No Company Benefit Plan provides benefits which are subject to taxation under Section 409A of the Code.

Section 409A governs the tax consequences of employer non-qualified deferred compensation plans. Such plans are generally exempt from federal income tax requirements until paid out to participants.

Section 4.16 Labor and Employment Matters.

(a) Schedule 4.16(a) sets forth a true, correct and complete list of (i) all employees (whether active, on leave, full-time, part-time or otherwise) of the Company, including all officers of the Company (collectively, the "Employees"); (ii) all current paid

consultants, dependent contractors or independent contractors engaged by the Company (collectively, the "Consultants"); and (iii) all retirees and terminated employees for which the Company has any benefits responsibility or other continuing or contingent obligation; together, in each case, with the following for each such Person, such Person's: (A) current rate of compensation or fees; (B) date of hire; (C) age; (D) title and/or job description; (E) part-time or full-time status; (F) accrued and unused vacation days; (G) accrued and unused sick days; (H) if on leave, the category and status of such leave (including expected return date); (I) location of employment; (J) the terms on which each of the Consultants are engaged; (K) employee benefit coverage selected; and (L) status as exempt or nonexempt from overtime under the FLSA (for only those Employees employed by the Company in the United States). Except as indicated on Schedule 4.16(a), all officers and employees of the Company are active.

Schedule 4.16 provides the buyer with a snapshot of the target company's labor force. It answers the basic question of: (a) how many full-time and part-time employees and contractors does the target company have; (b) what are the workforce's demographics, such as average age and gender composition; (c) what do they do; (d) how much do they get paid; and (e) how long have they been with the target company. Some sellers are reluctant to disclose this information either due to the sensitive nature of the compensation data or out of a concern that the buyer will attempt to solicit the target company's employees if the transaction fails to close. In their defense, buyers need this information to determine the target company's level of potential risk under state and federal employment laws. For example, an analysis of the workforce's gender composition and comparative earnings alerts a buyer to potential Equal Pay Act or gender discrimination liability. Further, this detailed employee information allows buyers to discover if there are any cost-saving synergies from employee overlap and for integration planning. There are several ways to bridge this disconnect. One is to release Schedule 4.16 on a "no names" basis, identifying employees by title only. Another is to password protect the schedule and release it only to the buyer's HR specialists/consultants on a "need to know" basis until closing.

> **(b) Except as set forth on Schedule 4.16(b), the Company is not a party to, or otherwise bound by, any Employment Agreement. The Seller has made available to the Buyer true, correct and complete copies of each Employment Agreement set forth on Schedule 4.16(b). Each such Employment Agreement is legal, valid and binding of the Company and enforceable against the Company in accordance with its terms. There is no existing default or breach by the Company under any Employment Agreement to which it is a party (or event or condition that, with notice or lapse of time or both could constitute a default or breach thereunder) and there is no such default, or event or condition that, with notice or lapse of time or both, could constitute a default or breach) with respect to any third party to any Employment Agreement to which the Company is a party.**

Companies have differing policies on employment agreements. There are some companies where every employee executes an employment agreement of some sort and there are others where only the executive officers of the company or just the CEO have employment agreements. Section 4.16(b) requires the seller to identify, and provide copies of, all employment agreements to the buyer. The representation and warranty continues to state that all these employment agreements are binding, in full force and effect, and have not been breached by the target company or the counterparties. Seller's counsel should be cautious in agreeing to represent or warranty to the binding nature or absence of breach of agreements with respect to the employees (which is arguably not within the target company's or the seller's knowledge or control). Consequently, many sellers will attempt to soften this representation and warranty by the addition of a knowledge qualifier. This information is essential for buyers to determine the extent and nature of the company's outstanding obligations to its employees and officers, which can be significant. For example, an incumbent CEO may have an employment agreement that does not allow for termination without a high standard of cause or payment of a large severance package. Such agreements are typically binding upon successors, and can place extreme limitations on a buyer's ability to manage and control the direction of a newly acquired company.

> **(c) The Company has not (and has not received a claim from any Governmental Entity to the effect that the Company has) (i) improperly classified as an independent contractor any officer or employee of the Company or (ii) improperly classified an employee as "exempt" or "non-exempt" under the FLSA or any state, local or foreign counterpart.**

Section 4.16(c) is a statement that the target company has not miss-categorized any employee or contractor or received any claim from a government entity to such effect. Counsel for a buyer should consider the misclassification of any group of employees or contractors to inevitably result in a collective action under the FLSA or state law equivalent, which can be crippling to a company's operating budget. Further, misclassification of any significant number of employees or contractors is used by labor unions as a leverage point to seek an election, or to bring unfair labor practice claims against employers with represented units of employees.

> **(d) Except as set forth on Schedule 4.16(d): (i) the Company is not a party to any collective bargaining agreement, contract or legally binding commitment to any trade union or employee organization or group in respect of or affecting employees; (ii) the Company is not engaged in any negotiation with any trade union or employee organization; (iii) the Company has not engaged in any unfair labor practice within the meaning of the NLRB, and there is no pending or, to the Knowledge of the Seller, threatened complaint regarding any alleged unfair labor practices as so defined; (iv) there is no strike, labor dispute, work**

> **slow down or stoppage pending or, to the Knowledge of the Seller, threatened against the Company; (v) there is no grievance or arbitration proceeding arising out of or under any collective bargaining agreement which is pending or, to the Knowledge of the Seller, threatened against the Company; (vi) the Company has not experienced any material work stoppage; (vii) the Company is not the subject of any union organization effort; and (viii) the Company is (and has been) in compliance with all applicable Labor Laws.**

Section 4.16(d) is focused on the target company's union relationships or pending risk of union organization. Certain sectors of the US economy (e.g. automobile, railroad, and steel industries) have heavy unionization while other have almost none at all. If the target company falls into one of the former areas, a labor specialist should be engaged to carefully scrutinize the target company's labor relations and practices. If, however, the target company is not in one of these sectors then the representation and warranty will less important. A common misconception among non-unionized employers is the belief that the National Labor Relations Act has no impact on their business. To the contrary, the NLRA applies to all employers, whether or not there is any union representation activity within their workforce. Accordingly, the representation in this subsection (viii) regarding compliance with all labor laws provides assurance to buyers that there is no present risk with regard to NLRA violations.

> **Section 4.17 Insurance Policies. Schedule 4.17 sets forth a true, correct and complete list of all policies of insurance carried by or for the benefit of the Company during the [___ (__)]-year period ended on the date hereof (each, an "Insurance Policy"), specifying the insurer, the amount of and nature of coverage, the policy limits or amounts of coverage, the deductible amount (if any), the annual premiums with respect thereto, and the date through which coverage will continue by virtue of premiums already paid. Each Insurance Policy (a) is in full force and effect, (b) is**

valid and binding in accordance with its terms, and (c) will continue in effect after the Closing Date. During the past [___ (__)] years, there has been maintained for the benefit of the Company insurance coverage that is substantially similar to the coverage set forth in the Insurance Policies. The Company has not (i) received notice of any cancellation or non-renewal or threat of cancellation or non-renewal of any Insurance Policy, (ii) reached or exceeded its policy limits for any Insurance Policy, (iii) failed to give any notice of any claim under any Insurance Policy in due and timely fashion, or (iv) been denied or turned down for coverage under any Insurance Policy.

Most corporations carry a number of insurance policies in the ordinary course of business. These may include general liability, directors and officers, errors and omissions, automobile insurance, and umbrella policies. Certain businesses such as airlines and builders may carry industry specific policies. Section 4.17 requires the seller to identify all insurance policies that are maintained by or on behalf of the target company, together with their policy limits, deductibles, and other specifics. This disclosure allows the buyer to get a picture of the target company's claim coverage and to what degree, if any, the target company self-insures. The representations and warranties in Section 4.17 also give the buyer assurance that such insurance policies will be in full force and effect when it takes control of the target company on the closing date and that similar policies have been in place since a mutually agreed historical date certain. Lastly, the representation and warranty confirms that the target company has not exceeded its policy limit, received any notice of non-renewal or denial of coverage. A buyer may further require that the seller provide a claims history of the target company for a certain period of time prior to closing.

Section 4.18 Environmental, Health and Safety Matters. Except as set forth on Schedule 4.18:

There is an expansive tapestry of state and federal laws and local ordinances regarding environmental compliance. Among other things, these laws cover the disposal of hazardous waste, certain discharges into bodies of water and certain emissions into the air. They often impose joint and several liability, include criminal charges in addition to civil charges, cover both direct and indirect violations and impose successor liability. A complete discussion of environmental laws is beyond the ambit of this book. That being said, a potential violation by the target company or any of its officers, employees, or agents is a very serious issue that could result in material liabilities for the buyer that could exceed the amount of the purchase price. One must, however, keep in mind that not every transaction poses the same environmental risk. Therefore, a buyer's counsel must assess on a case-by-case basis what degree of environmental scrutiny is required based on the facts and circumstances of the target company's business. If the buyer's counsel believes that a particular transaction has environmental risk, he or she should advise the buyer to engage environmental consultants to conduct an environmental analysis, which may include a Phase I and Phase II environmental site assessment. We have set out some factors below that should be viewed as red flags of potential environmental risk.

Authors Note: Environmental Risk Red Flags.

- The company owns real estate.
- The company leases real estate where the landlord is not a large commercial real estate company.
- The company is a manufacturing concern.
- The company is an agricultural concern.
- The company sells or leases physical products.
- The company is a waste disposal or transportation company.
- The company is a common carrier or owns/leases automobile, watercraft, or airplanes.

(a) the Company possesses all Permits and approvals required under, and is in compliance in all material respects with, all Environmental Laws, and the Company is in compliance in all material respects with all applicable limitations, restrictions, conditions, standards, prohibitions, requirements, obligations, schedules and timetables contained in all Environmental Laws or contained in any other Law, or any notice or demand letter issued thereunder;

Under environmental laws, certain companies are required to obtain permits due to the nature of their business. For example, (1) the Resource Conservation and Recovery Act (RCRA)[1] requires companies that treat, dispose of and store hazardous waste to obtain a federal permit from the Environmental Protection Agency; (2) The Clean Water Act requires companies that discharge dredge or fill materials into navigable waters to obtain a permit from the Army Corps of Engineers; and (3) The Clean Air, requires companies that emit certain pollutants into the atmosphere obtain permits from the state authorities.

Similar to the representation and warranty set forth in Section 4.12(b) regarding permits generally, Section 4.18(a) is a representation and warranty by the seller that the target company has all permits required under environmental laws and is in compliance with all such permits and all such laws. Note, these permits should be disclosed on Schedule 4.12(b). As discussed above in the Author's Note to Section 4.12, the reason that a separate representation and warranty with respect to environmental laws and permits is given is because the potential magnitude of the liability is such that it will likely be carved out from any limits of liability under the indemnification provisions agreed by the parties.

> **(b) the Company has not received notice of actual or threatened liability under CERCLA or any similar foreign, state or local Law from any Governmental Entity or any third party, and there is no fact or circumstance that could form the basis for the assertion of any claim against the Company under any Environmental Law, including CERCLA or any similar local, state or foreign Law with respect to any on-site or off-site location;**

CERCLA or the Comprehensive Environmental Response, Compensation and Liability Act of 1980[2], commonly known as "Superfund," is a federal law relating to the cleanup of hazardous waste sites. Section 4.12(b) is a representation and warranty by the seller that the target company has not received any notice or claim alleging any liability under CERCLA or any other

[1] Pub. L. No. 94-580, 90 Stat. 2795 (1976) (codified at 42 U.S.C. §§ 6901 *et seq.*).
[2] Pub. L. No. 95-510, 94 Stat. 2767 (1980) (codified at 42 U.S.C. §§ 9601 *et seq.*).

environmental law and that no fact or circumstance exists that could give rise to such a claim. Such an assurance is especially important because CERLCA imposes strict liability not only on the individual or entity that caused the hazardous waste condition, but also upon all subsequent owners of the property, even innocent purchasers who are unaware of any toxic condition.

> **(c) the Company is not subject to any Loss, contingent or otherwise, incurred or imposed or based upon any provision of any Environmental Law or arising out of (i) any act or omission of the Company, or an employee, agent or representative of the Company or (ii) the ownership, use, control or operation by the Company of any facility, site, area or property (including any facility, site, area or property currently or previously owned or leased by the Company) from which any Hazardous Material was Released; and**

Section 4.18(c) is a representation and warranty that the target company is not subject to any loss arising from a breach of environmental laws. This should be read together with the representation and warranty contained in the last sentence of 4.18(d) that the target company has not paid any fine or penalty arising from an environmental matter during a mutually agreed period prior to closing. The existence of any such loss or claim should be treated by the buyer with caution as it could signal the existence of facts or circumstances that could give rise to future environmental liability.

> **(d) the Seller has made available to the Buyer true, correct and complete copies of all reports, correspondence, memoranda, computer data and the complete files relating to the Company's environmental matters; and the Company has not paid any fine, penalty or assessment during the past [____ (__)] years with respect to environmental matters.**

Section 4.18(d) requires the seller to confirm that it has provided all correspondence and reports regarding environmental matters. This is intended to provide the buyer with comfort that they have received all information necessary to conduct environmental due diligence of the target company.

Section 4.19 Intellectual Property.

Intellectual property (IP) is a class of intangible assets that are recognized as proprietary under applicable laws. These assets generally cover patents, trademarks, copyrights, and trade secrets. Outside the United States, they also commonly cover the "moral rights" of a creator in a work. Depending on the target company's business, intellectual property may be the most important asset that it owns and the impetus for the buyer's desire to consummate the transaction. If this is the case, the buyer's counsel may want to engage specialists in intellectual property to conduct patent valuations, claims analysis, and audits of proprietary software.

(a) Schedule 4.19(a) sets forth a true, correct and complete listing of all Company Registered Intellectual Property, which identifies that which is owned and that which is licensed by the Company.

Certain classes of intellectual property can be registered with the United States Patent and Trademark Office (USPTO), or with respect to trademarks, the USPTO and/or state authorities with jurisdiction under state law (often the secretary of state). These include inventions, copyrights, and trademarks. Section 4.19(a) requires the seller to disclose in a schedule all such registered IP owned or licensed to the target company. Please note that not all companies register their entire portfolio of IP, because registration requires disclosure that may erode the value of the intellectual property. Consequently, Schedule 4.19(a) is unlikely to cover all IP used in the business.

(b) No Company Intellectual Property or product or service used by the Company related to Company Intellectual Property is subject to any Action or Order (i) restricting in any manner the use, transfer or licensing thereof by the Company, or (ii) that may affect the validity, use or enforceability of the Company Intellectual Property or any such product or service. Each item of Company Registered

Intellectual Property is valid and subsisting. All necessary registration, maintenance and renewal fees currently due or due within the next twenty (20) days in connection with Company Registered Intellectual Property have been made and all necessary documents, recordations and certifications in connection with the Company Registered Intellectual Property have been filed with the relevant patent, copyright, trademark or other authorities in the United States or foreign jurisdictions, as the case may be, for the purpose of maintaining such Company Registered Intellectual Property.

Company intellectual property covers all IP, owned or licensed by the target company, including any registered intellectual property. Section 4.19(b) is a statement by the seller that the IP used or necessary for use by the target company is not the subject of any lawsuit, claim, or order that restricts its use, transfer, or licensing or may affect its validity or enforceability. The representation and warranty then goes on to state that the target company has made all filings and payments necessary for maintaining the registered company IP and such registered company IP is valid and subsisting. Seller's counsel may notice that by grouping licensed intellectual property with owned intellectual property, this representation and warranty requires the seller to represent and warranty to matters that are beyond its knowledge and control (e.g., the validity of licensed company registered intellectual property and the absence of actions and orders regarding licensed company IP). Consequently, the seller's counsel may desire to reword the representation and warranty to separate and differentiate the treatment of the two.

(c) **The Company owns and has good and exclusive title to, or has licenses sufficient for the conduct of the Business as currently conducted and as proposed to be conducted to, each item of Company Intellectual Property, free and clear of any Lien, excluding licenses and related restrictions. The Company is the exclusive owner or exclusive licensee of the trademarks and service marks, trade names and domain names used by**

the Company, including the sale of any products or the provision of any services of the Company, free and clear of all Liens.

Similar to the "Title to Assets" representation and warranty set forth in Section 4.07, here the seller is representing and warranting that the target company has exclusive title or licenses that are sufficient for the operation of the business as conducted or as it is proposed to be conducted, to each item of company IP. Sometimes a buyer will seek to expand this representation and warranty by adding the following sentence to close the loop and ensure that the company IP captures the entire universe of intellectual property necessary for the operation of the business:

The Company Intellectual Property constitutes all of the Intellectual Property necessary or used to conduct the business and operations of the Company, as presently, previously or currently contemplated to be operated.

In each case, seller's counsel will be reluctant to give representations and warranty regarding the operation of the company post-closing and will likely move to limit the prospective application of the representation and warranty by removing the language regarding "current contemplation" and/or "proposed to be conducted."

The last sentence of this representation and warranty distinguishes trademarks and domain names from other IP and requires the seller to confirm that the target company has exclusive rights to such items.

(d) The Company owns exclusively and has good title to all copyrighted works used by the Company that (i) are products of the Company, or (ii) the Company otherwise expressly purports to own, free and clear of all Liens. Schedule 4.19 (d) lists all works of original authorship used by the Company and prepared by or on behalf of the Company (including software programs) by title, version number, author(s) and publication date, if any,

regardless of whether the Company has obtained or is seeking a copyright registration for such works.

Copyright law protects original works of author-ship that are fixed in a tangible medium.[3] Among other things, this covers "literary works" that have been held to include computer programs.[4]

> **Author's Note:**
> **Works of Authorship**
> (17 U.S.C. § 102):
>
> **Works of Authorship include:**
>
> (1) literary works;
> (2) musical works;
> (3) dramatic works;
> (4) pantomimes and choreographic works;
> (5) pictorial, graphic, and sculptural works;
> (6) motion pictures and other audiovisual works;
> (7) sound recordings; and
> (8) architectural works.

Section 4.19(d) includes a representation and warranty that the target company has exclusive title to all copyrighted works used by it that are products of the target company or that the target company otherwise purports to own. This representation and warranty also requires the seller to schedule all software and other works of authorship used by the target company.

Due to the broad compass of works of authorship as defined by the Copyright Act, the seller's counsel may desire to limit this representation and warranty by reference to materiality. This schedule will also need to cross-reference the target company proprietary software disclosed pursuant to Schedule 4.20(a).

(e) To the extent that the Company Intellectual Property has been developed or created by a third party for the Company, the Company has a written Contract with such third party with respect thereto and the Company thereby either

---

[3] 17 U.S.C. § 102 (West).
[4] *Apple Computer, Inc. v. Franklin Computer Corp.*, 714 F.2d 1240 (3d Cir. 1983).

(i) has obtained ownership of and is the exclusive owner of, or (ii) has obtained a license sufficient for the operations of the Business as currently conducted and as proposed to be conducted to, all of such third party's Intellectual Property in such work, material or invention by valid assignment.

Author's Note: The "Work for Hire" Doctrine and the "Hired to Invent" Doctrine:

The "Work of Hire" Doctrine is a rule set forth in the federal Copyright Act that states employers will be deemed to be the legal author/owner of copyrightable works of authorship created by an employee within the scope of his or her employment. (17 U.S.C. § 201(b) (West)).

The "Work for Hire" Doctrine does not apply to ownership of patentable inventions, which fall within the universe of state common law. Courts will generally require an employee to assign inventions to his or her employer when the employee was hired for the specific purpose of inventing (*Standard Parts Co. v. Peck*, 264 U.S. 52 (1924)). This common law rule is referred to as the "hired to invent doctrine." The application of the hired to invent doctrine to independent contractors differs greatly by jurisdiction.

These days, with increased globalization, it is not uncommon for corporations to outsource their software development needs to offshore development shops in India, Russia, Costa Rica or some other en vogue foreign country. However, if the corporation does not require the developer to execute documents expressly transferring all IP rights in the contracted work product to the corporation, then the corporation can end up in an uncomfortable position where the contractor, not the corporation, owns the software that it was paid to develop. Corporations sometimes erroneously rely on a presumption that the Work for Hire Doctrine will transfer the legal title of the works to them by operation of law. Unfortunately, the Work for Hire Doctrine does not apply to contractors unless there is a written agreement to the contrary, which expressly assigns the contractor intellectual property rights to the target company.

Section 4.19(e) is intended to give the buyer assurances that the target company has good title to all IP developed for the target company by third parties. The seller represents and warrants that the target company has written agreements with all its third-party developers of IP and that such agreements include an assignment or license sufficient for the target company to conduct its business as it is currently conducted or proposed to be conducted. As discussed above, the seller's counsel will likely desire to push back on the prospective nature of this representation and warranty.

If the business involves IP that is critical to the operation of the business and is developed internally by target company employees, then the buyer may want to add the following language to the representation and warranty:

> ***All employees of the Company have executed invention assignment/work for hire agreements assigning to the Company all such Person's right, title and interest in any inventions, works of authorship, developments and other Intellectual Property, invented, developed or reduced to practice by such Person during the term of their employment with the Company and relating to the Company or the Business.***

If any current or former key employee of the target company has not executed such an assignment agreement, then the buyer should consider requiring the seller to obtain and deliver signed agreements for those individuals as a condition to closing the transaction.

> **(f) The operations of the Business as currently conducted and as proposed to be conducted, including the Company's design, development, marketing and sale of the products or services of the Company, including with respect to products currently under development, has not and does not infringe, violate or misappropriate in any manner the Intellectual Property of any third party or constitute unfair competition or trade practices under the Laws of any jurisdiction.**

Section 4.19(f) is a representation and warranty that the business as currently conducted and as proposed to be conducted by the target company does not infringe the IP rights of any third party. As discussed above, the seller's counsel will likely push back on the prospective nature of this representation and warranty.

(g) The Company has not received written notice, and to the Knowledge of the Seller, there is no other overt threat, from any third party, that the operation of the Business as it is currently conducted and as proposed to be conducted, or any act, product or service of the Company, infringes, violates or misappropriates the Intellectual Property of any third party or constitutes unfair competition or trade practices under the Laws of any jurisdiction.

Section 4.19(g) is a representation and warranty that the target company has not received any notice alleging that its business, or any of its products or services, infringe the IP of any third party.

(h) To the Knowledge of the Seller, no Person has infringed, violated or misappropriated or is infringing, violating or misappropriating any Company Intellectual Property.

Section 4.19(h) is a representation and warranty that, to the seller's knowledge, no third party is infringing any of the target company's IP.

(i) The Company has taken reasonable steps to protect their rights in the Confidential Information and any trade secret or confidential information of third parties used by any Acquired Company, and, without limiting the generality of the foregoing, the Company has enforced a policy requiring each employee and contractor to execute a proprietary information/confidentiality agreement in substantially the form provided to the Buyer, and, except under confidentiality

obligations to which the receiving parties are bound, the Company has disclosed any Confidential Information or any such trade secret or confidential information of third parties.

Certain proprietary information of a company may be awarded protection under state trade secret laws if it meets the statutory standards set forth in the applicable jurisdiction. To obtain this protection, most states require that the information not be known to the public and subject to reasonable efforts to maintain such secrecy. Along these lines, Section 4.19(i) includes a representation and warranty that the target company's proprietary information is subject to reasonable efforts to prevent disclosure and/or misappropriation and that the target company has required its employees and contractors to execute standard non-disclosure agreements (in a form delivered to the buyer) for the purpose of protecting such information.

Author's Note. Definition of a Trade Secret:

The Uniform Trade Secret Act (National Conference of Commissioners on Uniform State Laws) (amended 1985), which as of the date hereof has been adopted by a majority of the states in the United States, defines a trade secret as follows:

"Trade secret" means information, including a formula, pattern, compilation, program, device, method, technique, or process, that:

(i) derives independent economic value, actual or potential, from not being generally known to, and not being readily ascertainable by proper means by, other persons who can obtain economic value from its disclosure or use, and
(ii) is the subject of efforts that are reasonable under the circumstances to maintain its secrecy (USTA §1.4)

Section 4.20 Software.

(a) Schedule 4.20(a) sets forth a true, correct and complete list of (i) the Company Proprietary Software, (ii) the Company Licensed Software, and (iii) all technical and restricted materials relating to

the acquisition, design, development, use or maintenance of computer code program documentation and materials used by the Company.

Section 4.20(a) is a disclosure representation and warranty, which requires the seller to list all software that is developed by or on behalf of the target company, on the one hand, and all software that is licensed to the target company by third parties, on the other hand. The buyer should review these schedules to confirm that all inbound licenses have been reviewed for relicensing and change of control provisions. Buyer's counsel will also want to consult with the buyer's technology expert to ensure that there are sufficient seat/processor licenses to cover the target company's current and planned usage.

(b) The Company has all right, title and interest in and to all Intellectual Property rights in the Company Proprietary Software. The Company has developed the Company Proprietary Software through its own efforts, and for its own account, and the Company Proprietary Software is free and clear of all Liens other than Permitted Liens. The use of the Company Software does not breach any material term of any license or other Contract between the Company and any third party. The Company is in compliance with the terms and conditions of all license agreements in favor of the Company relating to the Company Licensed Software.

Section 4.20(b) is a representation and warranty that the target company has good title to its propriety software and such software was developed by the target company through its own efforts. Given that company proprietary software, as works of authorship and company IP, falls within the ambit of Section 4.19(d) and (e) above, the comments to such sections are also applicable here.

The last sentence in Section 4.20(b) contains a representation and warranty that the target company is in compliance with all license agreements. A seller will likely desire to qualify this statement by materiality or material adverse effect to avoid a "foot-fault" breach of this representation and warranty. In some instances, where the target company licenses significant amounts of expensive software packages, the buyer may consider adding the following language to this representation and warranty:

> ***The consummation of the transactions contemplated by this Agreement and the ancillary documents hereto will neither violate nor result in the breach, modification, cancellation, termination or suspension under the terms and conditions of any Contracts, licenses or agreements relating to the Company Software. Following the Closing Date, the Company will be permitted to continue to exercise all of its rights under such Contracts, licenses and agreements to the same extent had the transactions contemplated by this Agreement not occurred and without the payment of any additional amounts or consideration other than ongoing fees, royalties or payments which the Company would otherwise be required to pay in the Ordinary Course.***

This will give the buyer additional protection against relicensing fees.

> **(c) the Company Proprietary Software does not infringe any patent, copyright or trade secret or any other Intellectual Property right of any third party. The source code for the Company Proprietary Software has been maintained in confidence.**

Similar to the representation and warranty in 4.19(f) regarding the non-infringement of third-party intellectual property generally, this representation and warranty focuses on the non-infringement of third party IP by target company proprietary software in particular.

> **(d) The Company Proprietary Software was: (i) developed by the Company's employees working within the scope of their employment at the time of such development; (ii) developed by agents,**

consultants, contractors or other Persons who have executed appropriate instruments of assignment in favor of the Company as assignee that have conveyed to the Company ownership of all of its Intellectual Property rights in the Company Proprietary Software; or (iii) acquired by the Company in connection with acquisitions in which the Company obtained appropriate representations, warranties and indemnities from the transferring party relating to the title to the Company Proprietary Software. The Company has not received notice from any third party claiming any right, title or interest in the Company Proprietary Software.

Please see the commentary to 4.19(e) above regarding Work for Hire.

(e) The Company has not granted rights in the Company Software to any third party.

This is a relatively straightforward representation and warranty that the target company has not granted rights in its software to any third party. Please note that if the target company is a software development company or a software service provider, an exception may need to be included for licensing/relicensing of its software to its customers, clients, and end-users in the ordinary course of business.

Section 4.21 Transactions with Affiliates. Except as set forth Schedule 4.21, no Company Affiliated Person has any interest in: (a) any Contract with, or relating to, the Company or its properties or assets; (b) any loan, arrangement, understanding or Contract for or relating to the Company or its properties or assets; or (c) any property (real, personal or mixed), tangible or intangible, used by the Company. Schedule 4.21 also sets forth a true, correct and complete list of all accounts receivable, notes receivable and other receivables and accounts payable owed to or due from any Affiliate of the Company to or from the Company.

It is not uncommon for a company to have commercial dealings with its stockholders, affiliates, or other related parties. A company with various operating subsidiaries that comprise a large consolidated group will often have contractual arrangements between and among the various subsidiaries, which are commonly referred to intercompany arrangement. A small company owned by one or very few owners might utilize in its operations assets owned by the owners, such as office space or, when in need of additional capital, might borrow money from an owner or family member of an owner in the form of a loan. The risk to a buyer is that these transactions were not negotiated on an "arm's-length" basis and might therefore be off-market to the detriment of the company. For that reason, a buyer should fully understand and evaluate each of these relationships prior to closing the transaction. Section 4.21 is a representation and warranty that requires the seller to disclose all contracts, agreements, arrangements, receivables, and payables between the company, on one hand, and any affiliated person, on the other hand. If upon review, the buyer determines that any of these arrangements are detrimental to the ongoing business of the company, then it should request that, as a condition to closing, it be terminated without any further liability to the company.

> **Section 4.22 Undisclosed Payments. Neither the Company nor any of its or directors, nor anyone acting on behalf of any of them, has made or received any payment not correctly categorized and fully disclosed in the Company's books and records in connection with or in any way relating to or affecting the Company.**

The accounting provisions of the Foreign Corrupt Practices Act of 1977 (FCPA) require issuers of stock traded on national securities exchanges to maintain books and records that accurately reflect such issuers' transactions.[5] The intent of this provision is to ensure that no off-balance sheet payments are being made to foreign officials in violation of the FCPA. In this vein, Section 4.22 is a representation and warranty by the seller that neither the target company nor any person acting on behalf of the target company has made or received any payment that is not correctly categorized and disclosed in the target company's books and records.

---

[5] 15 U.S.C. §§ 78dd-1 *et seq.* (West).

If the target company has substantial business in foreign countries, or in countries with high levels of corruption, the buyer should consider including more robust FCPA provisions, such as the following:

> ***Neither the Company, the Stockholders nor any of their Affiliates, nor any other Person acting on any of their behalf has, directly or indirectly, given or agreed to give any gift or similar benefit to any employee of a Government Entity or any other Person who is or may be in a position to help or hinder the Business or operations of the Company (or to assist the Company in connection with any actual or proposed transaction) which (a) might subject the Company, the Buyer or any of their respective Representatives, to any damage or penalty in any civil, criminal or other suit, investigation or action, (b) if not given in the past, might have had an adverse effect on the Business or operations of the Company, or (c) if not continued in the future, might adversely affect the Business, operations, cash flows or prospects of the Company, or which might subject the Company, the Buyer or any of their respective Representatives, to any damage or penalty in any civil, criminal or other suit, investigation or action.***

Any attempt by the seller to negotiate any material provision of the FCPA representation and warranty should be a red flag to the buyer.

> **Section 4.23 Customer and Supplier Relations.**
>
> **(a) Schedule 4.23(a) sets forth a true, correct and complete list of the names and addresses of the Customers, and the amount of sales to each Customer during the twelve (12)-month period ending [__________, 20__]. The Company maintains good relations with the Customers and, to the Knowledge of the Seller, no event has occurred that could adversely affect the Company's relations with any Customer in any material respect. Except as set**

> **forth in Schedule 4.23(a), no Customer during the prior twelve (12) months has canceled, terminated or made any threat to cancel or otherwise terminate any of such Customer's relations with the Company or to decrease in any material amount such Customer's usage of the Company's services or products. No Customer has notified the Company that such Customer will terminate or materially alter its business relations with the Company, either as a result of the Transactions or otherwise.**

Section 4.23 requires the seller to disclose a list of the target company's customers with revenue above a certain mutually agreed threshold (set forth in the definition of "customer"), together with the twelve-month trailing sales revenue for each such customer. If the buyer is a competitor of the target company, the seller may resist disclosure of customer details out of concern that the buyer will use the information for a competitive advantage if the deal does not close. The buyer, however, will desire to understand customer concentration for targeting high-value customer contracts for additional scrutiny, and for the purpose of gauging overall deal risk (customer concentration increases the impact of customer attrition). The buyer will also want to understand whether there are substantial overlaps between the buyer's and the target company's customer bases, which could lead to negative synergies in regulated businesses where a customer is required to maintain multiple vendors.

A common solution to this disclosure problem is for the seller to disclose a customer list with the names of the customer redacted or identified as customer 1, customer 2, customer 3, and so on. These identifiers would be keyed to the customer contracts, which in a sensitive competitive transaction, are also commonly redacted. To address overlap issues, a non-redacted customer list can be provided to the buyer's outside financial advisors for the limited purpose of creating an overlap analysis on a no-names basis.

The second part of the representation and warranty is directed at providing the buyer comfort regarding the stability of the target company's customer base and associated revenue. In particular, the seller represents and warrants that no events have occurred that could lead a customer to terminate or alter its relationship with the target company, and no customer has indicated an intent to terminate or diminish its relationship with the target company as a result of the transaction. Lastly, the seller represents and warrants that no customer has canceled, or threatened to cancel its relationship with the target company in the last twelve months. The buyer should investigate any disclosed cancellations to ensure that they were not a result of ongoing issues with target company services or products that could lead to future terminations.

Please see the commentary to Section 4.13(a)(xvi) for additional information regarding a target company's relationship with its customers.

> **(b) Schedule 4.23(b) sets forth a true, correct and complete list of the names and addresses of the Suppliers, and the annualized amount of purchases from each Supplier during the twelve (12)-month period ending [________ __, 20__]. The Company maintains good relations with the Suppliers and, to the Knowledge of the Seller, no event has occurred that could adversely affect the Company's relations with any Supplier in any material respect. Except as set forth on Schedule 4.23(b), no Supplier (or former Supplier) during the prior twelve (12) months has canceled, terminated or, to the Knowledge of the Seller, made any threat to cancel or otherwise terminate any of its Contracts or commitments with the Company or to decrease its supply of any services or products. No Supplier has notified the Company that such Supplier will terminate or materially alter such Supplier's business relations with any of the Company, either as a result of the Transactions or otherwise.**

Section 4.23(b) follows the same pattern as Section 4.32(a) but addresses the target company's supplier relationships. Generally, the supplier relationships are not as sensitive as customer relationships and do not result in the same issues surrounding disclosure. Please see Section 4.13(a)(xv) for additional information regarding a target company's relationship with its suppliers.

Section 4.24 Brokers, Finders and Investment Bankers. The Buyer will not be directly or indirectly obligated to pay or bear (e.g., by virtue of any payment by or obligation of the Company at or at any time after the Closing) any brokerage, finder's or other fee or commission to any broker, finder or investment banker in connection with the Transactions or any of the transactions contemplated by the Company Ancillary Documents or Seller Ancillary Documents based on arrangements made by or on behalf of the Company, except as specifically provided herein.

This "brokers, finders, and investment bankers" representation and warranty guarantees that the buyer will not be responsible for any of the target company's investment banker or broker's fees in connection with the transaction. It is important to determine whether the seller or the target company has engaged an investment banker or broker in connection with the transaction. It is not uncommon that the seller will engage an investment banker or broker at the target company level, which absent this representation could result in the buyer being responsible for such fees as the new owner of the target company. Considering that brokerage fees can be hundreds of thousands and even millions of dollars, a cautious buyer may require all such fees to be settled at closing out of the purchase price proceeds.

Section 4.25 Disclosure. None of the information supplied by or on behalf of the Company to the Buyer, and no representation, warranty or covenant made by the Seller in this Agreement or any Seller Ancillary Document or by the Company in any Company Ancillary Document contains an untrue statement of a material fact or omits to state a material fact required to be stated herein or therein or necessary to make the statements contained herein or therein not misleading. The financial projections relating to the Company delivered to the Buyer are made in good faith and are based upon reasonable assumptions, and the Seller is not aware of any fact or set of circumstances that could lead the Buyer to believe that such projections are incorrect or misleading in any material respect.

Among mergers and acquisitions (M&A) practitioners, this representation and warranty is typically referred to as "10b-5 rep." It derives its name from Rule 10b-5 of the Securities Exchange Act of 1934, as amended. Rule 10b-5 generally prohibits any act or omission resulting in fraud or deceit in connection with the purchase or sale of any security. Both the SEC and private citizens can enforce the requirements of the rule through lawsuits claiming monetary damages resulting from the alleged fraud or deceit. M&A practitioners have converted this concept of prohibiting fraud and deceit into a representation and warranty that applies to the sale of a business. More specifically, M&A practitioners representing buyers have adopted paragraph (b) of Rule 10b-5 into a representation and warranty that generally requires a seller to affirmatively state that it has not told the buyer any material untruths or failed to tell the buyer something that would make misleading the statements the seller did make to the buyer. This type of representation and warranty is usually not acceptable to a sophisticated seller. A seller will often tell the buyer that it has given access to all the due diligence information the buyer has requested and has answered, or had the executive officers answer, all the buyer's questions to its satisfaction. The seller will also argue that purchasers of publicly traded securities typically do not have deep access to nonpublic information, unfettered access to ask questions of executive officers of the issuer, or the ability to negotiate representations, warranties, or indemnities with the issuer; therefore, it is appropriate for the government to

> **Author's Note: Rule 10b-5: Employment of Manipulative and Deceptive Practices provides that:**
>
> It shall be unlawful for any person, directly or indirectly, by the use of any means or instrumentality of interstate commerce, or of the mails or of any facility of any national securities exchange,
>
> (a) To employ any device, scheme, or artifice to defraud,
> (b) To make any untrue statement of a material fact or to omit to state a material fact necessary to make the statements made, in the light of the circumstances under which they were made, not misleading, or
> (c) To engage in any act, practice, or course of business which operates or would operate as a fraud or deceit upon any person, in connection with the purchase or sale of any security. 17 C.F.R. § 240.10b-5.

step in and protect the interest of the public. Finally, a seller will argue that this type of representation and warranty is unfair from a seller's perspective and that the buyer should ultimately get comfortable with the state of the business based on its due diligence investigation of the business and the specific representations and warranties it has negotiated with the seller in the definitive purchase agreement. Nonetheless, a buyer will often attempt to get a seller to make this representation and warranty if for nothing else than to just have one bargaining chip to use in negotiations.

ARTICLE V
REPRESENTATIONS AND WARRANTIES OF THE BUYER

The Buyer hereby represents and warrants to the Seller as follows as of the Closing Date:

Buyer's representations and warranties in a stock purchase agreement tend to be limited to the "fundamental representations and warranties" (organization, authorization, absence of conflicts) and representations regarding investment bankers, and are generally not heavily negotiated. The idea being that the buyer's primary obligation under the purchase agreement is to pay the purchase price. If the transaction is structured with a delay between signing and closing, an additional representation regarding sufficiency of financing may be added to the buyer's representations. Further, if the buyer will be using stock in addition to, or in lieu of, cash to pay the purchase price, then the seller will likely request representations and warranties regarding the stock and the business operations of the buyer.

Section 5.01 Organization. The Buyer is a corporation duly organized, validly existing and in good standing under the Laws of the State of Delaware and has all requisite corporate power and authority to own, lease and operate its properties and to carry on its business as now being conducted.

This is a fundamental representation whereby the buyer represents that it is duly organized and in good standing. It is the counterpart to the representations and warranties regarding organization made by the seller and the company in Articles III and IV.

> **Section 5.02 Authorization. The Buyer has full power and authority to (a) execute and deliver this Agreement and each Buyer Ancillary Document, (b) perform its obligations under this Agreement and each Buyer Ancillary Document, and (c) consummate the transactions contemplated by this Agreement and each Buyer Ancillary Document. This Agreement and each Buyer Ancillary Document has been duly executed and delivered by the Buyer, and each of them constitutes the valid and binding agreement of the Buyer, enforceable against the Buyer in accordance with their respective terms, subject to applicable bankruptcy, insolvency, reorganization, moratorium or other similar Laws affecting the enforcement of creditors' rights generally, general equitable principles and the discretion of courts in granting equitable remedies.**

Similar to the authorization representations regarding the sellers and the company set forth in Articles III and IV, this is a fundamental representation regarding the buyer that you will find in almost every commercial transaction. It basically states that the buyer has the authority to undertake the transaction and to sign all the documents and perform all the obligations that are required to consummate the transactions contemplated by the definitive agreement.

> **Section 5.03 Absence of Restrictions and Conflicts. The execution and delivery of this Agreement and the Buyer Ancillary Documents, the consummation of the transactions contemplated hereby and thereby and the fulfillment of, and compliance with, the terms and conditions hereof and thereof do not or shall not, as the case may be, with the passing of time or the giving of notice or both, violate or conflict with, constitute a breach of or default under, result in the loss of any benefit under, or permit the acceleration of any obligation under, (a) any term or provision of the Buyer's Organizational Documents, (b) any Contract to which the Buyer is a party, (c) any Order to which**

the Buyer is a party or by which the Buyer or any of its properties is bound, or (d) any Law applicable to the Buyer.

Section 5.03 states that the execution of the agreement and purchase and sale of stock contemplated thereby will not violate any contracts to which the buyer is a party, the buyer's constitutional documents, or applicable laws.

Section 5.04 Brokers, Finders and Investment Bankers. None of the Sellers will be directly or indirectly obligated to pay or bear (e.g., by virtue of any payment by or obligation of the Buyer at or at any time after the Closing) any brokerage, finder's or other fee or commission to any broker, finder or investment banker in connection with the Transactions or any of the transactions contemplated by the Buyer Ancillary Documents based on arrangements made by or on behalf of the Buyer.

This brokers, finders, and investment bankers representations guarantees that the seller will not be responsible for any of the buyer's investment banker or broker's fees in connection with the transaction. In private company transactions, it is not as common for a buyer to engage an investment banker as it is for the seller to engage one. There are, however, instances where

ARTICLE VI
CERTAIN COVENANTS AND AGREEMENTS

Section 6.01 Public Announcements. Neither Party shall make any public announcements regarding this Agreement or the Transactions, including any announcements to the financial community, any Governmental Entity, any employees of the Company, any customers or suppliers of the Company or the general public, without the prior written consent of the other Party; provided, however, that the foregoing prohibition shall not apply to any announcement that is

required by Law, in which case the Party required to make such announcement shall use its commercially reasonable efforts to deliver to the other Party a copy of the same before such announcement is made.

This covenant regarding public announcements is intended to force the parties to cooperate on all public announcements regarding the transaction. The buyer will often revise this covenant so it is unilateral in its application to the seller. This position is premised on the buyer's need to freely communicate to customers, employees, and suppliers post-closing in the ordinary course of business. In the context of material transactions involving one or more publicly traded companies, it may be appropriate to enlarge the exception regarding disclosure in accordance with applicable laws to cover disclosures required by the rules of a national securities exchange on which such party's shares are listed, which may be more expansive than state and federal securities laws.

Section 6.02 Seller Release. In consideration for the agreement and covenants of the Buyer set forth in this Agreement, the Seller, on its own behalf, and on behalf of each of its Affiliates, hereby knowingly, voluntarily and unconditionally releases and forever discharges from and for, and covenants not to sue the Buyer, the Company, or any predecessor, successor, parent, subsidiary or other Affiliate of the Buyer or the Company, or any of their respective current and former officers, directors, employees, agents, or representatives for or with respect to, any and all claims, causes of action, demands, suits, debts, obligations, liabilities, damages, losses, costs, and expenses (including attorneys' fees) of every kind or nature whatsoever, known or unknown, actual or potential, suspected or unsuspected, fixed or contingent, that the Seller has or may have, now or in the future, arising out of, relating to, or resulting from any act of commission or omission, errors, negligence, strict liability, breach of contract, tort, violations of law, matter or cause whatsoever from the

beginning of time to the Closing Date; provided, however, that such release shall not cover: (a) any claims against the Buyer or any of its Affiliates (other than the Company) unrelated in any way to the Company or (b) any claims against the Buyer arising under this Agreement, any Seller Ancillary Document or any Buyer Ancillary Document.

It is customary in stock deals for the selling stockholders to execute broad agreements to waive and release the buyer and the target company from all claims, except claims that arise under the stock purchase agreement or are unrelated to the target company. The rationale for this waiver is rooted in the pre-existing relationship of the stockholders and the target company, the buyer's assumptions in valuing the target company, and the selling stockholders' receipt of consideration in the form of the purchase price. The pre-closing relationship between the target company and the selling stockholders may include the occurrence of certain facts and circumstances that could give rise to a claim for damages under applicable law. A critical assumption of the buyer in valuing the target company is that it is free and clear of any liabilities except those that are disclosed in the schedules to the purchase agreement. Selling stockholders vis-à-vis the buyer are in a unique position to assess at the time of closing whether any such claims exist. Accordingly, it is appropriate for the selling stockholders to give such a release at the closing. Seller's counsel should ensure that the exceptions set forth above are included in the release (not all the buyer form purchase agreements include this language). An aggressive seller's counsel could also attempt to limit the release to the target company on the grounds that the above justification applies only to the target company and not the buyer, especially if the seller has separate business dealings with the buyer or any of the buyer's affiliates.

Section 6.03 Cooperation Following the Closing. Following the Closing, each Party shall deliver to the other Party such further information and documents and shall execute and deliver to the other Party such further instruments and agreements as such other Party reasonably requests to consummate or confirm the Transactions, to accomplish the purpose of this

> **Agreement or to assure to such other Party the benefits of this Agreement.**

Section 6.03 is an agreement among the parties to take such actions and execute such documents after the closing as are needed to effect to the purchase and sale of the stock contemplated by the stock purchase agreement. This type of covenant is viewed as a "catch-all" provision and is common in all types of commercial agreements. This type of covenant is rarely negotiated in any depth. Occasionally, one of the parties, usually the buyer, will add clarifying language stating that no additional consideration is required to be delivered in connection with such actions. Similarly, it is not uncommon for one of the parties, usually the seller, to qualify the commitment to that of using "commercially reasonable efforts."

> **Section 6.04 Non-Competition.**
>
> **(a) The Stockholders hereby acknowledge that (A) the Company currently conducts, has plans to conduct or previously has conducted Business Activities (as defined below) throughout the Territory and (B) to adequately protect the interest of Buyer in the Company, it is essential that any non-compete covenant with respect thereto cover all of the Business Activities and the entire Territory and (C) part of the Purchase Price was allocated as to compensate the noncompetition obligations of Stockholders. "Business Activities" means any line of business throughout the Territory which the Company (1) is presently engaged on the Closing Date, (2) was previously engaged in the five (5) year period preceding the Closing Date, or (3) as of the Closing Date, has written plans to enter. So there may be no doubt, Business Activities shall include, without limitation, any kind of activities that are directly or indirectly, related to [(v) credit reporting, business reporting, (w) personal information solutions, (x) credit data marketing services, (y) identification management and (z)**

> **analytics and the development of solutions, as such relates to any of the foregoing.] "Territory" shall mean the States of [Georgia, Florida, Alabama, North Carolina and South Carolina.]**

A non-compete covenant is an agreement of the seller not to compete with the target company for a certain period following the closing. These restrictions typically cover competition through "ownership or operation" of a competing business or the provision of services to a competing business. Non-competition agreements are customary in most M&A transactions. The exception to this rule tends to be where the seller is a private equity or venture capital fund and has acted primarily as a passive equity holder. In these circumstances, the private equity or venture capital seller is often willing to agree only to a very limited non-compete or non-solicitation agreement.

While as a general matter, there is a strong juridical prejudice against non-compete agreements insofar as they constitute agreements in restraint of trade, in the sale of business context they are largely enforceable as long as they are reasonable in scope and duration. This exception recognizes that the seller, because of its ownership and operation of the target business, is in possession of confidential and proprietary information as well as "know-how" that would allow it to unfairly compete with the buyer post-closing, which essentially would prevent the buyer to receive the contemplated benefit of the bargain from the transaction. Further, in making this exception, courts recognize that non-compete agreements protect the buyer's legitimate business interest in "ring fencing" the financial projections of the target, which are often the basis of the discounted cash flows analysis underpinning purchase price.

Even though generally recognized as enforceable in nearly every jurisdiction in the United States, non-compete agreements are required to be narrowly tailored with respect to scope, geography, and duration, and are evaluated for reasonableness on a case-by-case basis. In some states, courts will reform or "blue pencil" a non-compete that is overly broad. Other states take a more draconian position whereby overly broad restrictions render the entire non-compete covenant void. Accordingly, it is important for a practitioner to carefully research the state law of the applicable jurisdiction to understand the substratum of enforceability prior to drafting the non-competition covenant.

<u>Territory.</u> The territorial restriction is not generally negotiated that much with both focusing on those jurisdictions in which the target company does business as of the closing date. The buyer should also seek to include any jurisdictions in which the target company does not currently operate but has current plans to enter.

<u>Business Activities</u>. The parties will need to define the type of business activities that the seller is prohibited from engaging. The language set forth in the example above is a very broad, buyer-friendly approach for defining the line of business. You will note that not only does it cover any activity in which the target company is currently engaged, but it also covers activities in which the target company was previously engaged or has plans to engage in the future. The definition goes on from there to describe the target company's business with more specificity to ensure that nothing is missed.

A sophisticated seller will try to narrow this as much as possible. Seller's strategy will be to negotiate a definition that specifically describes the business as it is currently conducted. This means that seller would strike everything except the last sentence of the definition and focus on the accuracy of this statement and whether there is anything that needs to be carved out from the definition (i.e., activities that are arguably competitive but that the seller intends to continue to conduct post-closing). Such an exception is often necessary where the seller is a strategic entity or owns several businesses in adjacent spaces that are not being transferred as part of the deal.

A seller-friendly approach will look something like this:

> "Business Activities" shall mean the business of marketing and selling to third parties [(x) credit reports, business reports, (y) credit data marketing services, and (z) identification management services; provided, that Business Activities shall not include the development, marketing or sale of personal wealth indication indices, including, without limitation, indices of the type currently developed, marketed and sold by Corporation ABC.]

> **(b) During the five (5) year period following the Closing Date (the "Non-compete Period"), neither the Stockholders, nor any of their respective Affiliates or representatives (acting on their behalf), shall in any manner directly or indirectly, conduct Business Activities or offer products or services competitive therewith in the Territory or otherwise engage in, have an equity or profit interest in, or render services (of an executive, marketing, manufacturing, research and development, administrative, financial, or consulting nature) to any Person that conducts any of the Business Activities or offers products or services competitive therewith in the Territory.**

The duration of the non-compete agreement or "non-compete period" refers to the term of the negative covenant as measured from the closing date. While the maximum enforceable term varies by jurisdiction, it is common to see a non-compete period of three to five years under Delaware and New York law. It is probable that any term in excess of five years would be unenforceable.

As compared to the other features of a non-compete covenant, it has been our experience that duration is most sensitive to the economic terms of the underlying deal. That is, while the scope and territory are often a matter of fact reflecting a snapshot of the target company's operation at closing, duration is prospective and therefore more susceptible to bargaining asymmetries among the parties. The greater the portion of a purchase price a particular seller is receiving or the more robust the valuation, the more willing it will be to sign up for a non-compete covenant with a longer term. If, however, there are multiple sellers, and one or more is a minority stockholder that is not receiving a substantial amount of cash in purchase price (i.e., "walk away money"), such a minority stockholder seller will often (legitimately) push-back on the duration of the non-compete. For example, while a buyer can reasonably expect the founder of the target company who owns 95 percent of the outstanding shares of the target company and is receiving $60 million at closing to sign up for a five-year non-compete, the buyer cannot reasonably expect an employee cashing out stock options in the transaction, who will receive $300,000 at the closing, to sign up for the same term.

If there is significant disparity among the sellers in the number of shares being sold by each of them, then the non-compete agreement is often moved from the stock purchase agreement to stand-alone ancillary agreements of varying durations to be executed as a closing condition by those sellers receiving significant value in the transaction.

Author's Note: As a buyer arguing duration of non-competition covenants, it is often useful to look at the forecast period used in the discounted cash flow analysis. If the forecast period is longer than the five years, which it often is, it is helpful to bring this fact to the seller's attention and make the argument that it is in fact getting paid not to compete for this period. Any unfair competition during this period would impact projections and thus decrease purchase price.

ARTICLE VII
INDEMNIFICATION

At the most basic level, an indemnity is an agreement by one party to hold another person harmless from certain claims and losses suffered by the indemnified party. Unlike contractual remedies, an indemnity claim does not require a breach of contract and unlike a tort claim, an indemnity claim does not generally require fault of the indemnifying party. Consequently, indemnification is generally thought of as providing more expansive protection than the remedies available under law.

Indemnification provisions are common in all types of commercial transactions and customary in change of control transactions where a private company is the target. The contrary is true with respect to transactions where a public company is the target or transaction involving a distressed or bankrupt target company, which rarely include indemnification provisions.

Article VII sets forth the terms and conditions pursuant to which the seller agrees to indemnify the buyer, and vice versa. As risk-shifting provisions, with potential significant economic impact, the terms and conditions of indemnification are generally the subject of lengthy negotiations between the parties. In negotiating indemnification provisions, it is helpful to review deal studies published annually by third parties such as the American Bar Association, which set forth reported deal statistics on material contract terms including, indemnification, caps, baskets and claims periods. Due to the nature of deal reporting these studies tend to have a small sample set which is skewed toward larger deals and is consequently more seller-favorable than may be warranted with smaller transactions that often involve more deal risk.

> **Section 7.01 Indemnification Obligations of the Seller. The Seller shall indemnify, defend and hold harmless the Buyer Indemnified Parties from, against, and in respect of, any and all Losses arising out of or relating to:**

Section 7.01 sets forth the seller's indemnity obligations to the buyer. As such, it can be thought of as answering the question of "what happens if the buyer does not get what it bargained for in the transaction?" The buyer is entering the transaction with an intent, and has valued the target company on the assumption that its assets are in good and usable condition, that it does not have any material liabilities, and that the seller will comply with certain customary covenants and agreements. These assumptions are captured in the representations and warranties, covenants and agreements made by the seller in the purchase agreement and the ancillary documents executed and delivered at closing. If those representations and warranties are not true, or the seller breaches an agreement or covenant, then the target company is not in the condition that the buyer bargained for. The intent of Section 7.01 is to enable a buyer to recapture this value. In this way, it can be thought of as a "money back guarantee."

Please see the introduction to Article IV for a discussion of joint and several liability when there are multiple sellers.

> **(a) any breach of or inaccuracy in any representation or warranty made by the Seller in Article III or Article IV of this Agreement, any Seller Ancillary Document or any Company Ancillary Document;**

Section 7.01(a) established the seller's obligation to indemnify the buyer for damages suffered by the buyer as a result of a breach of any representation or warranty set forth in Article III or IV of the purchase agreement or any ancillary document delivered by the seller at the closing. To recover under this section, the buyer will need to demonstrate that (1) an event has occurred or the existence or non-existence of certain fact or circumstances have become known to the buyer, and (2) that such an event, facts, or circumstances constitute a breach of the seller's representations or warranties.

Example: After the closing, the buyer performs an audit of the target company's accounts receivable and discovers that the target company factored $100,000 of its receivables and used the cash for off-balance sheet payments. This is minimally a breach of the representations and warranties set forth in Section 4.08(b) (Accounts Receivable) and Section 4.22 (No Undisclosed Payments), which has resulted in the buyer suffering $100,000 of direct damages. These damages would be recoverable under this Section 7.01(a).

> **(b) any claim asserted or held by any Person (against any Buyer Indemnified Party) that, if meritorious, would constitute or give rise to a breach of or inaccuracy in any representation or warranty made by the Seller in Article III or Article IV of this Agreement, any Seller Ancillary Document or any Company Ancillary Document;**

Section 7.01(b) can be distinguished from Section 7.01(a) in that it addresses breaches of representations and warranties in the context of third-party claims. To recover under this section, the buyer will need to demonstrate that (1) it has received a third-party claim (this can be either formal or informal) and (2) if such claim is true it would constitute a breach of one or more of the seller's representations or warranties. Unlike, Section 7.01(a), which triggers a payment obligation, Section 7.01(b) initially triggers a defense obligation that becomes a payment obligation only if the seller loses or settles the claim.

Example: After the closing, the buyer receives an e-mail from the target company's Oracle representative indicating that the target company must purchase three additional seat licenses to comply with its current licensure agreement. If true, this would, at least, constitute a breach of 4.19(c) (Intellectual Property). As a result, this claim would fall under the seller's defense and indemnification obligations set forth in Section 7.01(b).

Author's Note: In order for the buyer to make a claim pursuant to Section 7.01(a) or (b), there must have been a breach or inaccuracy of a representation or warranty made by the seller in the transaction documents. If the seller has disclosed a liability on the disclosure schedules as an exception to such representation then no breach exists. For the buyer to receive indemnity for disclosed liabilities a specific indemnity such as the following should be added:

> ***any liability arising from or relating to any matter disclosed on the [Schedules 4.11 (Legal Proceedings)], [____________] to this Agreement.***

This type of specific indemnity is common when the seller discloses material outstanding litigation or other contingent liabilities that cannot be easily quantified and taken into account when valuing the company prior to closing.

> **(c) any breach by the Seller of any covenant, agreement or undertaking made by the Seller in this Agreement, any Seller Ancillary Document or any Company Ancillary Document;**

Section 7.01(c) sets forth the seller's obligation to indemnify the buyer for damages arising from any breach by the seller of any of its covenants or agreements contained in the purchase agreement or any ancillary documents thereto. To recover under this section, the buyer must demonstrate that (1) an event has occurred or the existence or non-existence of certain facts or circumstances have become known to the buyer and (2) that such event, facts, or circumstances constitute a breach of one or more of the seller's agreements or covenants contained in the transaction documents.

Example: After the closing, the seller opens a new business in direct competition with the target company. The target company promptly loses its largest customer to the seller's new business. This would constitute a breach of the seller's non-competition agreements set forth in Section 6.04. Consequently, the buyer would be entitled to claim remuneration for monetary damages arising from such breach pursuant to this Section 7.01(c) in addition to any action at equity to enjoin the seller's competitive activities.

> **(d) any liability or obligation relating to claims by any Person relating to any equity interest in the Company or purported equity interest in the Company granted prior to the Closing Date; or**

Section 7.01(c) sets out line item indemnification covering any claims by any person relating to the equity interest in the target company. This is analogous to the "right of quite enjoyment" that commonly appears in real estate transactions, where a real estate seller agrees to protect the buyer against any claims by others that they own the subject property. Here the seller is agreeing to defend and hold the buyer harmless from any claims by a third party who purports to own capital stock or other equity securities of the target company. Note that this indemnity would be additional to the coverage that would otherwise be available under 7.01(b) for a breach of the seller's representations and warranties as to the target company's capitalization set forth in Section 4.03 and the seller's title to the shares set forth in Section 3.03. The justification for this double coverage arises from the essential nature of the equity to the transaction, and the line item indemnification streamlines recovery by removing the requirement that the buyer demonstrate a breach of representation or warranty.

Example: Following the closing, the buyer receives a letter from the seller's estranged husband in Texas claiming that the seller's transfer of 50 percent of the shares was invalid because they were rightfully owned by him under state property law and, therefore, the buyer must pay the estranged husband the purchase price that the buyer already paid to his estranged wife. Because the claim relates to a purported equity interest in the target company, the buyer would be entitled to indemnification pursuant to this Section 7.01(c) without the need to show a breach under any representation or warranty.

> **(e) any liability of any of the Company (i) for any Taxes of the Company with respect to any Tax period or portion thereof ending on or before the Closing Date (or for any Tax period beginning before and ending after the Closing Date to the**

extent allocable to the portion of such period beginning before and ending on the Closing Date), and (ii) for the unpaid Taxes of any Person (other than the Company) under Treasury Regulations section 1.1502-6 (or any similar provision of state, local, or foreign law), as a transferee of successor, by contract, or otherwise.

The indemnity set forth in Section 7.02(e) is an apportionment of tax liability among the parties. Traditionally the seller is responsible for all taxes of the target company with respect to any tax period or portion thereof before the closing date and the buyer is responsible for any tax liability of the target company for any tax period or portion thereof after the closing date. This "line item" indemnity is necessary because in the absence of such a provision, all taxes of the target company, regardless of when incurred or payable, would be on the buyer's account as the new owner of the target company. It would be possible for the buyer to seek remuneration for unpaid taxes pursuant to a breach of Section 4.14 (Taxes; Tax Returns), however this would not cover allocation of any taxes for periods straddling the closing date. Further, similar to Section 7.01(c) standalone indemnification is justified on the grounds that the apportionment of taxes is so fundamental to the transaction that the buyer should not be required to demonstrate a breach of representation or warranty to obtain recovery.

Example. The buyer receives a letter from a state taxing authority post-closing alleging that the target company failed to withhold and remit sales tax for Internet sales within such state during certain pre-closing periods. Because this claim relates to a liability of the target company for pre-closing taxes, the buyer would be entitled to indemnity pursuant to this Section 7.02(e), in addition to any claims that it might have for breach of representation or warranty.

The Losses of the Buyer Indemnified Parties described in this Section 7.01 as to which the Buyer Indemnified Parties are entitled to indemnification are collectively referred to as "Buyer Losses".

Section 7.02 Indemnification Obligations of the Buyer. The Buyer shall indemnify and hold harmless the Seller Indemnified Parties from, against and in respect of any and all Losses arising out of or relating to:

Section 7.02 sets forth the buyer's obligations to indemnify the seller for certain losses arising from the transaction. Since the buyer's primary obligation under the agreement is to deliver the purchase price, buyers are generally unwilling to give any substantial indemnities. Contrast this with transactions structured as asset deals where the buyer assumes certain liabilities in connection with the transaction for which the seller will rightfully expect indemnification post-closing.

(a) any breach or inaccuracy of any representation or warranty made by the Buyer in Article V of this Agreement or any Buyer Ancillary Document; or

Section 7.02(a) sets forth the buyer's obligations to indemnify the seller for a breach of representation or warranty. The buyer's representations and warranties are generally limited to authorization, organization, and absence of conflicts. This indemnity, therefore, protects the seller against a claim that the buyer was not authorized to consummate the transaction or that in consummating the transaction, the buyer was in violation of applicable laws or a government order. In each case, the big risk is that the transaction will be unwound with the buyer returning the shares and the seller disgorging the purchase price.

(b) any breach of any covenant, agreement or undertaking made by the Buyer in this Agreement or any Buyer Ancillary Document.

Section 7.02(b) sets forth the buyer's obligations to indemnify the seller for a breach of covenant or agreement. This indemnity is limited in effect considering that the buyer typically does not undertake many obligations under the purchase agreement aside from delivering the purchase price at closing.

The Losses of the Seller Indemnified Parties described in this Section 7.02 as to which the Seller Indemnified

Parties are entitled to indemnification are collectively referred to as "Seller Losses".

Section 7.03 Indemnification Procedure.

The procedures set forth in this Section 7.03 describe the rules that the party seeking indemnity must follow to lodge a claim. As an overview, (1) Section 7.03(a) covers third party claims, (2) Section 7.03(b) covers settlement of third party claims and (3) Section 7.03(c) addresses claims for payment. If the parties have executed an escrow agreement in connection with the transaction, it is important to make sure that the claims processes under both documents are in harmony.

(a) A Buyer Indemnified Party or a Seller Indemnified Party, as the case may be (an "Indemnified Party") shall notify promptly the Buyer or the Seller, as the case may be (the "Indemnifying Party"), following such Indemnified Party's receipt of notice from a third party, including any Governmental Entity, of any Action (a "Third Party Claim") with respect to which such Indemnified Party may be entitled to receive payment from the Indemnifying Party for any Buyer Loss or any Seller Loss, as the case may be; provided, however, that an Indemnified Party's failure to so notify the Indemnifying Party will relieve the Indemnifying Party from liability under this Agreement with respect to such Third Party Claim only if, and only to the extent that, such failure to so notify the Indemnifying Party results in the forfeiture by the Indemnifying Party of rights and defenses that would have otherwise been available to the Indemnifying Party with respect to such Third Party Claim. The Indemnified Party's notice shall describe the Third Party Claim in reasonable detail to the extent practicable based upon the facts then known by the Indemnified Party, and shall indicate the amount (estimated, if necessary) of the Loss that has been or may be suffered. The Indemnifying Party shall have the

right, upon (i) delivering written notice to the Indemnified Party within fifteen (15) days after receiving notice of such Third Party Claim and (ii) assuming full responsibility for any Buyer Losses or Seller Losses, as the case may be, resulting from such Third Party Claim, to assume the defense of such Third Party Claim, including the employment of counsel reasonably satisfactory to the Indemnified Party and the payment of the fees and disbursements of such counsel. Notwithstanding the foregoing, the Indemnifying Party shall not have any right to assume the defense of any Third Party Claims if (x) such Third Party Claim relates to any Company Intellectual Property or any Governmental Entity, (y) such Third Party Claim seeks a finding of criminal liability of, equitable remedies against, or any judgment or term that in any manner affects, restrains or interferes with the business of, the Indemnified Party or any of the Indemnified Party's Affiliates, or (z) the Indemnified Party reasonably believes that the interests of the Indemnifying Party and the Indemnified Party with respect to such Third Party Claim are in conflict with one another, and as a result, the Indemnifying Party could not adequately represent the interests of the Indemnified Party in such Third Party Claim. If, however, the Indemnifying Party declines or fails to assume the defense of the Third Party Claim on the terms provided in the immediately preceding sentence or to employ counsel reasonably satisfactory to the Indemnified Party, in either case within such fifteen (15)-day period, then the Indemnifying Party shall pay the reasonable fees and disbursements of counsel for the Indemnified Party as incurred. In any Third Party Claim for which indemnification is being sought under this Agreement, the Indemnified Party or the Indemnifying Party, whichever is not assuming the defense of such Third Party Claim, shall have the

> **right to participate in such matter and to retain its own counsel at such Party's own expense. The Indemnifying Party or the Indemnified Party, as the case may be, shall at all times use reasonable efforts to keep the Indemnifying Party or Indemnified Party, as the case may be, reasonably apprised of the status of the defense of any matter the defense of which it is maintaining and to cooperate in good faith with each other with respect to the defense of any such matter, which cooperation shall include furnishing or causing to be furnished such records, information, and testimony (subject to any applicable confidentiality agreement), and attending such conferences, discovery proceedings, hearings, trials, or appeals as may be reasonably requested in connection therewith; provided, however, that neither the Indemnified Party nor the Indemnifying Party will be required to grant access to or furnish information to the other party or such other party's Representatives to the extent that such access or the furnishing of such information would result in the waiver of an attorney-client or attorney work product privilege; provided, that, in each such case, the Indemnifying Party or the Indemnified Party, as the case may be, shall identify to the other party in reasonable detail such withheld information and the basis for such non disclosure.**

As noted above, this section sets forth the process for indemnification with respect to third-party claims (e.g., a claim by a buyer pursuant to Section 7.01(b)). For purposes of simplicity, the material parts of this process can be broken down into the following steps:

1. The buyer or seller receives a third-party claim for which it is entitled to indemnification from the other party under the purchase agreement (e.g., third-party claims for payment, complaints in litigation, correspondence from a government agency, etc.)
2. The buyer or seller decide to seek indemnification hereunder (indemnified party) and sends a notice to the other party (indemnifying

party), which describes the nature and amount of the claim with reasonable particularity. Note, that failure to so notify the indemnifying party relieves such party from liability only if it results in a forfeiture by the indemnifying party of rights and defenses that would have otherwise been available with respect to such claim.

3. The indemnifying party has fifteen days after receiving the notice to accept responsibility and assume the defense of the claim, except in the following cases:

   a. The claim involves criminal liability, equitable remedies, or potential restriction on the business of the indemnified party;
   b. The claim relates to any company IP or any governmental entity; or
   c. The indemnified party reasonably believes that the interests of the indemnifying party and the indemnified party with respect to such claim are in conflict.

4. If the indemnifying party assumes defense of such claim then it must select counsel that is satisfactory to the indemnified party, and be responsible for all legal fees associated with engaging that counsel.
5. If the indemnifying party does not assume the defense of the claim (or is not entitled to assume the defense of such claim pursuant to 3(a)-(c)), then the indemnifying party must pay the costs and fees of the indemnified party's legal counsel to defend the claim.

(b) An Indemnified Party shall not settle or compromise any Third Party Claim or consent to the entry of any judgment with respect to any Third Party Claim, in each case, for which indemnification is being sought under this Agreement, without the prior written consent of the Indemnifying Party (not to be unreasonably withheld, conditioned or delayed), unless (i) the Indemnifying Party fails to assume and maintain the defense of such Third Party Claim pursuant to Section 7.03(a), or (ii) such settlement, compromise or consent includes an unconditional release of the Indemnifying Party and its officers, directors, employees and Affiliates from all liability

> **arising out of such Third Party Claim. An Indemnifying Party shall not, without the prior written consent of the Indemnified Party (not to be unreasonably withheld, conditioned or delayed), settle or compromise any Third Party Claim or consent to the entry of any judgment with respect to any Third Party Claim, in each case, for which indemnification is being sought under this Agreement, unless (x) such settlement, compromise or consent includes an unconditional release of the Indemnified Party and its officers, directors, employees and Affiliates from all liability arising out of such Third Party Claim, (y) does not contain any admission or statement suggesting any wrongdoing or liability on behalf of the Indemnified Party, and (z) does not contain any equitable order, judgment or term that in any manner affects, restrains or interferes with the business of the Indemnified Party or any of the Indemnified Party's Affiliates.**

Section 7.03(b) sets forth the restrictions on the indemnifying party and the indemnified party's right to settle or compromise a claim without the consent of the other party. The material provisions of these restrictions can be mapped out as follows:

1. *Settlement by Indemnified Party.* An indemnified party may settle a claim for which it seeks indemnification, without the consent of the indemnifying party only if:

    a. The indemnifying party had a right to assume the defense of the claim but failed to do so; or
    b. The settlement includes an unconditional release of the indemnifying party.

2. *Settlement by Indemnifying Party.* An indemnifying party that assumes the defense of a claim for which it is required to indemnify the other party may settle the claim without the consent of the indemnified party only if:

a. The settlement includes an unconditional release of the indemnified party;
b. The settlement does not contain any admission or statement suggesting wrong doing by the indemnified party; and
c. The settlement does not include an equitable order or other term that restricts or interferes with the business of the indemnified party.

(c) If an Indemnified Party claims a right to payment pursuant to this Article VII, such Indemnified Party shall send written notice of such claim to the appropriate Indemnifying Party. Such notice shall specify the basis for such claim. The failure by any Indemnified Party so to notify the Indemnifying Party shall not relieve the Indemnifying Party from any liability that it may have to such Indemnified Party with respect to any claim made pursuant to this Article VII, it being understood that notices for claims in respect of a breach of a representation or warranty must be delivered prior to the expiration of the Claims Period under Section 7.04. If the Indemnifying Party does not notify the Indemnified Party that the Indemnifying Party disputes its liability to the Indemnified Party under this Article VII or the amount thereof within thirty (30) days after it receives such notice, then the claim specified by the Indemnified Party in such notice shall be conclusively deemed a liability of the Indemnifying Party under this Article VII, and the Indemnifying Party shall pay the amount of such liability to the Indemnified Party on demand or, in the case of any notice in which the amount of the claim (or any portion of the claim) is estimated, on such later date when the amount of such claim (or such portion of such claim) becomes finally determined. If the Indemnifying Party has timely disputed its liability with respect to such claim as provided above, as promptly as possible, such Indemnified Party and

the appropriate Indemnifying Party shall establish the merits and amount of such claim (by mutual agreement, litigation, arbitration or otherwise) and, within five (5) Business Days after the final determination of the merits and amount of such claim, the Indemnifying Party shall pay to the Indemnified Party immediately available funds in an amount equal to such claim as determined under this Agreement.

Section 7.03(c) sets forth the process for indemnification with respect to claims for payment by an indemnified party which do not involved third party claims (e.g., claims for payment made by the buyer pursuant to Section 7.01(b)). For purposes of simplicity, the material parts of this process can be broken down into the following steps:

1. The indemnified party sends a written claim for payment to the indemnifying party, specifying with reasonable particularly the facts and circumstances giving rise to the claim.
2. The indemnifying party has a thirty-day period to review the claim and determine whether it will accept liability.
3. If the indemnifying party does not deliver a written notice to the indemnified party within such period disputing its liability, then the claim shall be conclusively deemed a liability of the indemnifying party.
4. If the indemnifying party does dispute its liability in such period, then the parties will resolve the claim by litigation (or arbitration).

Section 7.04 Claims Period. The Claims Periods under this Agreement shall begin on the date of this Agreement and terminate as follows:

The claims periods set forth the time limits during which an indemnified party may bring a claim for indemnification pursuant to the purchase agreement. As such, the periods can generally be considered a private or contractual statute of limitations that starts to run on the closing date. State laws differ on the enforceability of contractual provisions modifying the applicable statute of limitation. While contractual modification providing for claims periods that are shorter than the statute of limitations have been upheld by courts under Delaware law[6] those providing for claims periods longer than the statute of limitation have been ruled unenforceable as contrary to public policy.[7] Based on the foregoing, buyer's and seller's counsel should research the applicable laws of the anticipated jurisdiction of enforcement prior to drafting and negotiating this provision so that they can make informed decisions on risk allocation.

> **(a) with respect to Buyer Losses arising under (i) Section 7.01(a) or Section 7.01(b) with respect to any breach or inaccuracy of any representation or warranty in Section 3.01 (Authorization), Section 3.03 (Ownership of Company Shares), Section 3.05 (Brokers, Finders and Investment Bankers), and Section 3.06 (Amounts Owed to Sellers), Section 4.01 (Organization), Section 4.02 (Authorization), Section 4.03 (Capital Stock), Section 4.21 (Transactions with Affiliates), and Section 4.24 (Brokers, Finders and Investment Bankers) (collectively, the "Surviving Representations"), or (ii) Section 7.01(c) and (collectively, the "Surviving Obligations"), the Claims Period shall continue indefinitely;**

The group of representations and warranties identified in subsection (i) ((Section 3.01 (Authorization), Section 3.03 (Ownership of Company Shares), Section 3.05 (Brokers, Finders and Investment Bankers), Section 3.06 (Amounts Owed to Sellers), Section 4.01 (Organization), Section 4.02 (Authorization), Section 4.03 (Capital Stock), Section 4.21 (Transactions with Affiliates), and Section 4.24 (Brokers, Finders and Investment Bankers)) are commonly referred to as "fundamental representations" and are viewed as so basic and fundamental to the transaction that they receive special treatment for purposes of claims periods, baskets and caps. With respect to claims periods, this special treatment manifests itself as an indefinite period of time following the closing during which a buyer is permitted to make claims for breach. While the seller may initially resist this

---

[6] *See GRT, Inc. v. Marathon GTF Tech., LtD.*, CIV.A. 5571-CS, 2011 WL 2682898 (Del. Ch. July 11, 2011).

[7] *Shaw v. Aetna Life Ins. Co.*, 395 A.2d 384, 386-87 (Del. Super. 1978).

position as a straw man in a negotiation gambit (perhaps by suggesting that all claims should survive for an eighteen-month period), almost all purchase agreements when executed include an indefinite claims period for fundamental representations. Other representations and warranties may be considered for an indefinite claims period on a deal-by-deal basis.

As discussed above, an indefinite claims period may be unenforceable under applicable law insofar as it extends beyond the statute of limitations.

> **(b) with respect to Buyer Losses arising under (i) Section 7.01(a) or Section 7.01(b) with respect any breach or inaccuracy of any representation or warranty in Section 4.14 (Tax Returns; Taxes) (the "Tax Representations") or (ii) Section 7.01(e) (the "Tax Obligations"), the Claims Period shall continue until ninety (90) days after the expiration of any applicable statute of limitations relating to the rights of any third party to bring any claim with respect to such matters;**

Section 7.04(b) establishes a claims periods that is tied to the underlying statute of limitations for third-party claims. The types of losses included in this category tend to be governmental claims of a nature that could result in significant liability to the target company (i.e., tax, environmental and labor matters).

> **(c) with respect to Seller Losses arising under Section 7.02(a), the Claims Period shall continue indefinitely, except as limited by Law (including any applicable statutes of limitation); and**

Section 7.04(c) provides the counterpart to Section 7.04(a) and provides an indefinite claims period for claims by the seller that the buyer breached its "fundamental representations." As discussed above, an indefinite claims period may be unenforceable under applicable law insofar as it extends beyond the statute of limitations.

> **(d) with respect to all other Buyer Losses or Seller Losses arising under this Agreement, the Claims**

Period shall terminate on the date that is twenty-four (24) months after the Closing Date.

Section 7.04(d) establishes the default claims period for all losses that are not separately addressed in Sections 7.04(a)-(c). As you might imagine, the buyer and seller are in diametric opposition on the length of the default period. A seller desires to minimize its potential liability from the transaction to as short a period as possible. Conversely, the buyer wants to maintain its freedom to make claims for losses as they arise, for as long a period as possible. As a rule of thumb, the buyer should strive to have the default claims period cover at least one full financial statement audit cycle of the target company to flush out any potential losses; the theory being that most operational contingencies will manifest during this period or be uncovered in the process of auditing the target company's financial statements.

Notwithstanding the foregoing, if, prior to the close of business on the last day of the applicable Claims Period, an Indemnifying Party shall have been properly notified of a claim for indemnity under this Agreement and such claim shall not have been finally resolved or disposed of at such date, such claim shall continue to survive and shall remain a basis for indemnity under this Agreement until such claim is finally resolved or disposed of in accordance with the terms of this Agreement.

This provision clarifies that all claims made prior to the last day of the applicable claims period survive until fully and finally resolved. However, to understand the effect of this provision on a particular claim it is first necessary to understand the statute of limitation at law with respect to such claim. The risk being that, if a claim is made before the claim period ends, but no formal complaint is filed until after the statute of limitations has run, then the complaint may be time barred depending on the laws of the applicable jurisdiction regarding contractual modification of the statute of limitations.

Section 7.05 Liability Limits. The Buyer Indemnified Parties shall not make a claim for indemnification under Section 7.01 for Buyer Losses unless and until the

> **aggregate amount of such Buyer Losses exceeds [________ Dollars ($•)] (the "Basket"), in which case the Buyer Indemnified Parties may claim indemnification for the full amount of such Buyer Losses; provided, however, neither the Surviving Representations nor the Tax Representations shall be subject to the Basket.**

Section 7.05 sets forth certain upper and lower limitations on an indemnifying party's indemnification obligations pursuant to the purchase agreement. The first element of the limitation is determining at what amount of indemnifiable loss does an indemnifying party's indemnification obligation get triggered. Section 7.05, as drafted, provides for what is commonly referred to among practitioners as a "tipping basket." It establishes the threshold amount of indemnifiable losses that an indemnified party must suffer before it is entitled to make a claim for indemnification. With a tipping basket, once the indemnified party has incurred this threshold amount of losses it can recover the aggregate amount of all losses (going back to the first dollar of loss), not just losses in excess of the basket amount. This should be contrasted with a "true deductible" where only losses in excess of the threshold amount can be recovered. We have set out an example below to further illustrate the differences between these two alternatives.

<u>Example</u>: The buyer and seller agree in the purchase agreement on a tipping basket of $100,000. Three months after the closing, the buyer suffers software-related losses of $75,000 due to the target company's pre-closing over-licensing of Oracle software. While this loss is a result of a breach of the seller's representations and warranties in the purchase agreement, the buyer is unable to claim indemnification from the seller because the amount of the loss ($75,000) is less than the amount of the tipping basket ($100,000). Six months later, the buyer receives a letter from Sybase claiming that a recent software audit has revealed that the target company has been over-licensing its software for at least two years and needs to pay $60,000 for additional seat licenses. This claim, if true, would constitute a breach of the seller's representations and warranties. Because the basket has now been exceeded ($60,000 + $75,000 = $135,000 >$100,000), the buyer can claim the full $135,000 of losses from the seller. Note, however, that if this were a "true

deductible," the buyer would be entitled to recover only $35,000 from the seller, which is the amount in excess of the deductible amount.

Based on the example, you will probably not be surprised to learn that buyers generally prefer tipping baskets and sellers generally prefer true deductibles. The amount of the basket or deductible is usually pegged to a percentage of the purchase price, which is set based on "market practices," which in turn are often the subject of much debate among the parties. Generally, when embroiled in one of these disputes regarding what is "market," it is helpful to reference an objective source such as the American Bar Association's Private Target's Mergers & Acquisitions Deal Point Study. It is also useful to reframe the question to think about the materiality of a loss or losses as it relates to the company's annual EBITDA and revenue for the most recent fiscal year.

Once the value and character of basket or deductible is agreed, it is customary to agree that certain indemnifiable losses are not subject to the basket or deductible, meaning that the indemnifying party must indemnify the indemnified party without regard to whether the loss is an excess of the basket or the deductible, whatever the case may be. These "first dollar" losses almost always include losses resulting from fraud or willful misconduct, losses arising from the breach of a covenant, and losses arising from a breach of a fundamental representation. Such exclusion is premised on the argument that these losses were preventable by the indemnifying party or are of such a nature that an indemnified party should never be required to pay them. In addition to the fundamental representations and fraud or willful misconduct, it is not uncommon to see "carve outs" for representations and warranties regarding taxes, employee benefits, environmental matters and title to assets. Other representations and warranties may be excepted from the basket or the deductible on a case-by-case basis depending on the underlying details and nature of the target company's business and any particular liabilities or potential liabilities the buyer discovered in due diligence.

> **The total aggregate amount of the liability of the Seller for Buyer Losses shall be limited to [________ Dollars ($•)] (the "Cap"); provided, however, that the Surviving Obligations, the Surviving Representations, the Tax Obligations and the Tax Representations**

> **shall not be subject to the Cap; provided, further, that the total aggregate amount of liability of the Seller for Buyer Losses arising under Article VII with respect to any breach or inaccuracy of any of the Surviving Representations or Tax Representations, and the Surviving Obligations and the Tax Obligations shall be limited to an aggregate amount equal to the Purchase Price.**

The second element of the limits of liability set forth in Section 7.05 is what is often referred to as the "cap." If the basket or deductible can be visualized as establishing the floor for an indemnifying party's liability, the cap should be visualized as establishing the ceiling. Like the basket or the deductible, the cap can be expressed as a percentage of purchase price and sometimes, depending on the negotiation leverage, an indemnifying party can be liable for indemnifiable losses in excess of the cap amount, such as losses arising from fraud or willful misconduct and losses arising from a breach of a fundamental representation. Other exceptions to the cap are negotiated by the parties depending on the parties' respective leverage, and vary from deal to deal. A useful tool in bridging disputes between buyer and seller regarding the amount of the cap is to apply different caps to different claims—similar to the methodology for claim periods set forth above in Section 7.04. For example, under this methodology, a claim for breach of a representation with respect to software might be capped at 20 percent of the purchase price, while a claim for tax matters is capped at 50 percent of the purchase price and a claim for fraud or breach of essential representations is uncapped.

> **Section 7.06 Determination of Losses. In calculating the amount of any Buyer Losses arising from a breach of any representation, warranty or covenant contained in this Agreement which is qualified by the words "material," "in all material respects," "Material Adverse Effect" or similar terms, or by a specific dollar threshold, such Buyer Losses shall be calculated as if such qualifier or threshold were not contained therein, it being understood that the exclusion of such qualifier or threshold shall apply solely for the purpose of calculation of Buyer Losses, and not for the purpose of determining whether or not such a breach has occurred.**

This section is commonly referred to as a "materiality scrape" among M&A practitioners. The intent of the provisions is to avoid double counting materiality qualifiers in representations and warranties in determining the amount of any indemnifiable loss suffered by the buyer (it being understood that materiality in this regard is replaced by the basket or deductible). The seller should carefully review the application of the materiality scrape as applied to ensure that it does not unintentionally undermine the intention of any representations or warranties.

> **Section 7.07 Investigations. The respective representations and warranties of the Parties contained in this Agreement or any certificate or other document delivered by any Party at or prior to the Closing and the rights to indemnification set forth in this Article VII shall not be deemed waived or otherwise affected by any investigation made, or knowledge acquired, by a Party.**

Often the seller will attempt to include "anti-sandbagging" provisions in a purchase agreement for the purpose of disclaiming the seller's indemnification obligations for any liabilities that are "known" to the buyer. At first cut, this looks fair. Why should the buyer have the opportunity to pursue the seller for claims that were fully disclosed? The problem is with defining the universe of the buyer's knowledge. Did the buyer fully comprehend the risk posed by a disclosed liability or just have knowledge of superficial facts and circumstances of the matter giving rise to the risk? Further, the inclusion of anti-sandbagging provisions incentivizes the seller to game the system by over disclosing for the purpose of burying material liabilities in hopes that the buyer will miss the risk and assume the liability through constructive knowledge. Lastly, an anti-sandbagging provision can have the effect of requiring the buyer to prove that it had no knowledge of the underling liability as a *prima facie* component of making a claim for indemnity. Accordingly, it is important for the buyer to establish that knowledge will not affect its rights of recovery. Section 7.07 is a buyer-friendly provision that is antithesis of an anti-sandbagging clause in that it specifically states that the buyer's knowledge and due diligence investigations does and will not interfere or limit the buyer's right to make a claim for indemnification.

> **Section 7.08 Treatment of Indemnification Payments. All payments made pursuant to this Article VII shall**

be deemed adjustments to the Purchase Price for Tax purposes.

Section 7.08 clarifies that payments made in satisfaction of indemnification claims will be treated as adjustments to purchase price for tax purposes.

Section 7.09 Exclusive Remedies. Each Party acknowledges and agrees that, except for (a) any claim for injunctive or other equitable relief pursuant to Section 8.12 or (b) any claim related to any criminal activity, fraud or intentional misrepresentation by the other Party in connection with the Transactions, its sole and exclusive remedy with respect to any and all claims for any Legal Dispute shall be pursuant to the indemnification provisions set forth in this Article VII.

The exclusive remedies section effectively precludes the parties from seeking relief outside the "four corners" of the contract, except in the case of criminal activity, fraud, intentional misrepresentations, and equitable remedies. The rationale for this provision is that the indemnities have been fully negotiated and represent the agreement between the parties with respect to allocation of risk. As such, a party should not be able to elect to either pursue indemnification or in the alternative seek recovery under contract or tort theory if they think it will be more favorable. In particular, in the absence of an exclusive remedies provision, a buyer may be able to argue that the limits of liability are not intended to apply to an action at law for breach of contract or negligence. As a result, these provisions are usually not included in a buyer's first draft of the contract.

ARTICLE VIII
MISCELLANEOUS PROVISIONS

Section 8.01 Notices. All notices, communications, consents and deliveries under this Agreement shall be delivered in writing, unless otherwise expressly permitted herein, and shall be deemed given: (a) when delivered if delivered personally (including by courier); (b) on the third day after mailing, if mailed,

postage prepaid, by registered or certified mail (return receipt requested); (c) on the day after mailing if sent by a nationally recognized overnight delivery service which maintains records of the time, place and receipt of delivery; or (d) upon receipt of a confirmed transmission, if sent by telex, telecopy or facsimile transmission, in each case to the parties at the following addresses or to such other addresses as may be furnished in writing by one Party to the others:

To the Buyer: [________________]
[________________]
[________________]
Attn: [________________]
Fax: [________________]

with a copy to: [________________]
[________________]
[________________]
Attn: [________________]
Fax: [________________]

and

[________________]
[________________]
[________________]
Attn: [________________]
Fax: [________________]

To the Seller: [________________]
[________________]
[________________]
Attn: [________________]
Fax: [________________]

with a copy to: [________________]
[________________]
[________________]
Attn: [________________]
Fax: [________________]

Section 8.01 sets forth the methods under which legal notice may be delivered pursuant to the agreement and the dates on which they will be deemed to be effective. It should be noted that the form agreement allows delivery pursuant to e-mail, telex, and other electronic means. It is not uncommon to require legally effective notice to be delivered only by conventional delivery methods (courier, certified mail, national carrier, etc.) and allow for electronic courtesy copies that are not alone sufficient for legal notice. This decreases the risk associated with missing an e-mail or fax in the flurry of electronic communications which typifies today's business environment.

> **Section 8.02 Schedules and Exhibits. The Schedules and Exhibits are hereby incorporated into this Agreement and are hereby made a part of this Agreement as if set out in full in this Agreement.**

Section 8.02 integrates the schedules and exhibits into the purchase agreement by reference. This makes clear that the schedules and exhibits are part of the agreement and, therefore, should be construed in accordance with the agreement's terms. If there are any disputes that arise from any schedule or exhibit, then the terms of the agreement would govern how the parties must resolve those disputes.

> **Section 8.03 Assignment; Successors in Interest. No assignment or transfer by any Party of such Party's rights and obligations under this Agreement shall be made except with the prior written consent of the other Party; provided, however, that the Buyer shall, without the obligation to obtain the prior written consent of any other Party, be entitled to assign this Agreement or all or any part of its rights or obligations under this Agreement to any of the Buyer's Affiliates, any lenders for collateral or other purposes, or to any subsequent purchaser of all or substantially all of the stock or assets of the Acquired Companies; provided that no such assignment shall release the Buyer of its obligations under this Agreement. This Agreement shall be binding upon and shall inure to the benefit of the Parties and their**

respective successors and permitted assigns, and any reference to a Party shall also be a reference to the successors and permitted assigns thereof.

Section 8.03 is an anti-assignment clause that limits each party's right to assign its rights and obligations under the agreement. You will notice that it is drafted to allow the buyer to make certain assignments without the prior consent of the seller. This is usually the case where such assignments are customary and typically do not adversely affect any of a seller's rights or remedies under the agreement. Even if the permitted assignments are made, the buyer will typically remain primarily liable under the agreement for its obligations.

Section 8.04 Captions. The titles, captions and table of contents contained in this Agreement are inserted in this Agreement only as a matter of convenience and for reference and in no way define, limit, extend or describe the scope of this Agreement or the intent of any provision of this Agreement.

Section 8.04 clarifies that the titles, captions, and table of contents are for convenience only and have no legal significance. A court is, therefore, put on notice to interpret only the provisions in the agreement and to not attempt to draw any independent meaning from the titles, captions and table of contents in the agreement.

Section 8.05 Controlling Law; Amendment. This Agreement shall be governed by and construed and enforced in accordance with the internal Laws of the State of Delaware without reference to its choice of law rules. This Agreement may not be amended, modified or supplemented except by written agreement of the Parties.

Section 8.05 is a standard choice of law provision selecting Delaware law as the governing law of the agreement. Both Delaware and New York have well-developed bodies of corporate law and as a result are often selected as the governing law for stock purchase agreements and other M&A documents.

> Section 8.06 Consent to Jurisdiction, Etc. Each Party hereby irrevocably agrees that any Legal Dispute shall be brought only to the exclusive jurisdiction of the courts of the State of Delaware or the federal courts located in the State of Delaware, and each Party hereby consents to the jurisdiction of such courts (and of the appropriate appellate courts therefrom) in any such suit, action or proceeding and irrevocable waives, to the fullest extent permitted by Law, any objection that it may now or hereafter have to the laying of the venue of any such suit, action or proceeding in any such court or that they any such suit, action or proceeding that is brought in any such court has been brought in an inconvenient forum. During the period a Legal Dispute that is filed in accordance with this Section 8.06 is pending before a court, all actions, suits or proceedings with respect to such Legal Dispute or any other Legal Dispute, including any counterclaim, cross-claim or interpleader, shall be subject to the exclusive jurisdiction of such court. Each Party hereby waives, and shall not assert as a defense in any Legal Dispute, that (a) such Party is not subject thereto, (b) such action, suit or proceeding may not be brought or is not maintainable in such court, (c) such Party's property is exempt or immune from execution, (d) such action, suit or proceeding is brought in an inconvenient forum, or (e) the venue of such action, suit or proceeding is improper. A final judgment in any action, suit or proceeding described in this Section 8.06 following the expiration of any period permitted for appeal and subject to any stay during appeal shall be conclusive and may be enforced in other jurisdictions by suit on the judgment or in any other manner provided by applicable Laws.

Section 8.06 is a standard forum selection clause whereby the parties submit to exclusive jurisdiction of the state and federal courts of Delaware and prospectively waive defenses that such forum is inconvenient or otherwise inappropriate. This gives the parties some predictability as to where they will end up if disputes rise to the level of formal litigation.

Section 8.07 Severability. Any provision of this Agreement that is prohibited or unenforceable in any jurisdiction shall, as to such jurisdiction, be ineffective to the extent of such prohibition or unenforceability without invalidating the remaining provisions of this Agreement, and any such prohibition or unenforced-ability in any jurisdiction shall not invalidate or render unenforceable such provision in any other jurisdiction. To the extent permitted by Law, each Party hereby waives any provision of law that renders any such provision prohibited or unenforceable in any respect.

Section 8.07 sets forth the intent of the parties that any prohibited or unenforceable provision of the agreement be rendered ineffective without invalidating the remaining provisions of the agreement. For example, if a court were to find the non-compete unenforceable because its terms were over-reaching or otherwise outside of public policy, then the parties would still want the other provisions of the agreement to be upheld to the extent they are within the bounds of public policy.

Section 8.08 Counterpart Signature Pages; Electronic Delivery. This Agreement may be executed in multiple signature pages (including by means of telecopied or e-mailed signature pages), any one of which need not contain the signatures of more than one Party, but all such signature pages taken together shall constitute one and the same instrument. This Agreement and any signed agreement or instrument entered into in connection with this Agreement, and any amendments hereto or thereto, to the extent signed and delivered by means of a PDF email, shall be treated in all manner and respects as an original agreement or instrument and shall be considered to have the same binding legal effect as if it were the original signed version thereof delivered in person. At the request of any Party hereto or to any such agreement or instrument, each other Party hereto or thereto shall re-execute original forms thereof and

deliver them to all other Parties. No Party hereto or to any such agreement or instrument shall raise the use of a PDF email to deliver a signature or the fact that any signature or agreement or instrument was transmitted or communicated through the use of a PDF email as a defense to the formation of a contract and each such Party forever waives any such defense.

As noted in Article II, in today's Internet-based business environment closings are increasingly virtual with all signature pages and execution documents being delivered by way of e-mail or other electronic medium. Section 8.08 clarifies the intent of the parties that all such electronically delivered documents have the same significance and legal effect as manually executed documents delivered in person.

Section 8.09 Enforcement of Certain Rights. Nothing expressed or implied in this Agreement is intended, or shall be construed, to confer upon or give any Person other than the Parties, and their successors or permitted assigns, any right, remedy, obligation or liability under or by reason of this Agreement, or result in such Person being deemed a third-party beneficiary of this Agreement.

Section 8.09 clarifies that there are no third-party beneficiaries of the agreement. That is, only the parties to the agreement can enforce the terms of the agreement. There might be third parties who would benefit from the agreement being enforced or held invalid; however, this provision makes clear that neither party to the agreement is intending for any third parties to have any rights under the agreement. An agreement can provide for a third party to have rights under an agreement even though that third party is not a signatory to the agreement. If the parties desire to allow for this, then it is advisable that the parties clearly state it in the agreement.

Section 8.10 Waiver. Any agreement on the part of a Party to any extension or waiver of any provision of this Agreement shall be valid only if set forth in an instrument in writing signed on behalf of such Party. A

> **waiver by a Party of the performance of any covenant, agreement, obligation, condition, representation or warranty shall not be construed as a waiver of any other covenant, agreement, obligation, condition, representation or warranty. A waiver by any Party of the performance of any act shall not constitute a waiver of the performance of any other act or an identical act required to be performed at a later time.**

Section 8.10 requires that any waiver of any right under the agreement be in a signed writing. This provision is intended to set in place a clear process by which a party can effectively waive its rights so that there is no confusion between the parties in such an instance.

> **Section 8.11 Integration. This Agreement and the documents executed pursuant to this Agreement supersede all negotiations, agreements and understandings among the Parties with respect to the subject matter of this Agreement (except for that certain Confidentiality Agreement, dated as of [________ ___, 20__], by and between [______] and [______]) and constitute the entire agreement among the Parties with respect thereto.**

Section 8.11 is a "merger" clause, whereby the parties agree that the terms and conditions of the agreement supersede all other agreements and discussion of the parties with respect to the subject matter of the agreement. This provision makes clear that the terms of the transaction are located with the "four corners" of the agreement and the related schedules and exhibits; therefore, a court should not look outside those documents when attempting to interpret the deal or otherwise resolve any dispute between the parties.

> **Section 8.12 Specific Performance. Each Party acknowledges and agrees that the non-breaching Party would suffer irreparable damage if any provision of this Agreement were not performed in accordance with its specific terms or were otherwise breached.**

Accordingly, each Party agrees that, in the event of any breach or threatened breach by the other Party of any covenant or obligation contained in this Agreement, (a) the non-breaching Party shall be entitled (in addition to any other remedy that may be available to it whether in law or equity, including monetary damages) to seek and obtain (i) a decree or order of specific performance to enforce the observance and performance of such covenant or obligation, and (ii) an injunction restraining such breach or threatened breach, and (b) it will not assert, and hereby does, waive, in any action for specific performance, the defense of adequacy of a remedy at law. Each Party further agrees that neither the other Party nor any other Person shall be required to obtain, furnish or post any bond or similar instrument in connection with or as a condition to obtaining any remedy referred to in this Section 8.12, and each Party irrevocably waives any right it may have to require the obtaining, furnishing or posting of any such bond or similar instrument.

Section 8.12 is an agreement of the parties that a non-breaching party will be entitled to seek an equitable remedy from a court if the other party fails to perform any of its obligations under the agreement. This remedy allows a party to stop the other party in its tracks, in addition to seeking damages through indemnification, if the other party is not adhering to the terms of the agreement. For example, if a party is disclosing confidential details regarding the terms of the transaction in violation of Section 6.01 or if the seller is violating the terms of the non-compete covenant in Section 6.04, then the aggrieved party can petition the court for an injunction to require the breaching party to cease the activities that are being taken in violation of the terms of the agreement.

Section 8.13 Transaction Costs. Except as provided above or as otherwise expressly provided in this Agreement, (a) the Buyer shall pay its own fees, costs and expenses incurred in connection herewith and the

Transactions, including the fees, costs and expenses of its financial advisors, accountants and counsel, and (b) at the Closing, the Seller shall pay the fees, costs and expenses of the Seller and the Company incurred in connection herewith and the Transactions, including the fees, costs and expenses of their respective financial advisors, accountants and counsel.

Section 8.13 specifies that each party will be responsible for the fees and costs that it incurs in connection with the transaction. Further 8.13(b) requires the seller to pay its own transaction costs and those of the target company at the closing. This ensures that the buyer is not left with unpaid transaction fees of the target company that were incurred solely for the benefit of the seller.

ARTICLE IX
DEFINITIONS; CONSTRUCTION

Section 9.01 Definitions. The following terms, as used in this Agreement, have the following meanings:

"Acquisition" has the meaning given to such term in the recitals of this Agreement.

"Action" means any claim, suit, action, proceeding, arbitration, application, litigation, lawsuit, hearing, inquiry, complaint, charge or investigation by or before any Governmental Entity and any appeal from any of the foregoing.

"Affiliate" of any particular Person means any other Person controlling, controlled by or under common control with such particular Person. For the purposes of this definition, "control" means the possession, directly or indirectly, of the power to direct the management and policies of a Person whether through the ownership of voting securities, contract or otherwise.

"Agreement" means this Stock Purchase Agreement as the same may be amended, supplemented or otherwise modified from time to time, this "Agreement".

"Applicable Benefit Laws" means all Laws or other legislative, administrative or judicial promulgations, other than ERISA and the Code, including those of a jurisdiction outside the United State of America, applicable to any Company Benefit Plan or ERISA Affiliate Plan.

"Audited Financial Statements" has the meaning given to such term in (a).

"Balance Sheet" has the meaning given to such term in (a).

"Basket" has the meaning given to such term in 0.

"Buyer" has the meaning given to such term in the preamble of this Agreement.

"Buyer Ancillary Document" means any certificate, agreement, document or other instrument, other than this Agreement, to be executed and delivered by the Buyer in connection with the transactions contemplated by this Agreement.

"Buyer Indemnified Parties" means the Buyer and its Affiliates, each of their respective officers, directors, employees, agents and representatives and each of the heirs, executors, successors and assigns of any of the foregoing.

"Buyer Losses" has the meaning given to such term in 0.

"Business" has the meaning given to such term in the recitals of this Agreement.

"Business Day" means any day except Saturday, Sunday or any day on which banks are generally not open for business in New York, New York.

"Cap" has the meaning given to such term in 0.

"CERCLA" means the United States Comprehensive Environmental Response, Compensation and Liability Act and the rules and regulations promulgated thereunder.

"Claims Period" means the period during which a claim for indemnification may be asserted under this Agreement by an Indemnified Party.

"Closing" has the meaning given to such term in 0.

"Code" means the United States Internal Revenue Code of 1986, as amended.

"Company" has the meaning given to such term in the recitals of this Agreement.

"Company Affiliated Person" means (a) any stockholder, director or officer of the Company, (b) any individual with whom any stockholder, director or officer of the Company has any direct or indirect relation by blood, marriage or adoption (a "Family Member"), (c) any entity in which any stockholder, director or officer of the Company or any of his or her Family Members owns any beneficial interest (other than a publicly held corporation whose stock is traded on a national securities exchange or in the over-the-counter market and less than 5% of the stock of which is beneficially owned by all such stockholders, directors, officers and Persons in the aggregate), or (d) any Affiliate of any stockholder, director or officer of the Company or any of his or her Family Members.

"Company Ancillary Document" means any certificate, agreement, document or other instrument, other than this Agreement, to be executed and delivered by the Company in connection with the Transactions.

"Company Benefit Plan" means each Employee Benefit Plan sponsored or maintained or required to be sponsored or maintained at any time by the Company or to which the Company makes or has made, or has or has had an obligation to make, contributions at any time or with respect to which the Company has any liability, whether direct or indirect or contingent or otherwise.

"Company Intellectual Property" means any Intellectual Property that is owned by or licensed to the Company, including the Company Software.

"Company Leased Real Property" has the meaning given to such term in (a).

"Company Licensed Software" means all software (other than Company Proprietary Software) used by the Company.

"Company Owned Real Property" has the meaning given to such term in 0.

"Company Proprietary Software" means all software owned by the Company.

"Company Real Property" has the meaning given to such term in (a).

"Company Registered Intellectual Property" means all of the Registered Intellectual Property owned by, filed in the name of, or licensed to the Company.

"Company Shares" has the meaning given to such term in the recitals of this Agreement.

"Company Software" means the Company Licensed Software and the Company Proprietary Software.

"Confidential Information" means all non-public and all proprietary information relating to the Company or the Business, including, the terms of this Agreement and any related transactions.

"Contract" means any agreement, contract, commitment, lease, license, arrangement, consensual obligation, understanding, promise or undertaking, (whether written or oral and whether express or implied), whether or not legally binding.

Note that this definition includes oral agreements. If the target company has entered into material oral agreements, the buyer should consider requiring these to be memorized in writing prior to the closing. A more creative approach is to require the seller to summarize the material terms of an oral agreement in the disclosure schedule regarding contracts so that the seller gives representations and warranties with respect to that oral agreement.

"Customers" means each Person that is a customer of the Company as of the date of this Agreement that paid the Company in the aggregate more than $[•] during the twelve (12)-month period ended [__________, 20__].

"Disclosure Schedules" has the meaning given to such term in (f).

"Employee Benefit Plan" means, with respect to any Person, (a) each plan, fund, program, agreement, arrangement or scheme, including each plan, fund, program, agreement, arrangement or scheme maintained or required to be maintained under the Laws of a jurisdiction outside the United States of

America, in each case, that is at any time sponsored or maintained or required to be sponsored or maintained by such Person or to which such Person makes or has made, or has or has had any liability, whether direct or indirect or contingent or otherwise, with respect to, or any obligation to make, contributions providing for employee benefits or for the remuneration, direct or indirect, of the employees, former employees, directors, managers, officers, consultants, independent contractors, contingent workers or leased employees of such Person or the dependents of any of them (whether written or oral), including each deferred compensation, bonus, incentive compensation, pension, retirement, stock purchase, stock option and other equity compensation plan, "welfare" plan (within the meaning of Section 3(1) of ERISA, determined without regard to whether such plan is subject to ERISA), (b) each "pension" plan (within the meaning of Section 3(2) of ERISA, determined without regard to whether such plan is subject to ERISA), (c) each employment, change of control, severance plan or agreement, health, vacation, summer hours, supplemental unemployment benefit, hospitalization insurance, medical, dental, legal, and (d) each other employee benefit plan, fund, program, agreement, arrangement or scheme.

"Employment Agreement" means any employment Contract, consulting agreement, termination or severance agreement, change of control agreement or any other agreement respecting the terms and conditions of employment or payment of compensation, or of a consulting or independent contractor relationship in respect to any current or former officer, employee, consultant or independent contractor.

"Environmental Laws" means all local, state and federal Laws relating to protection of surface or ground water, drinking water supply, soil, surface or subsurface strata or medium, or ambient air, pollution control, product registration and Hazardous Materials.

"ERISA" means the United States Employee Retirement Income Security Act of 1974 and the rules and regulations promulgated thereunder.

"ERISA Affiliate" means any Person (whether incorporated or unincorporated) that together with any Acquired Company would be deemed a "single employer" within the meaning of Section 414 of the Code.

"ERISA Affiliate Plan" means each Employee Benefit Plan sponsored or maintained or required to be sponsored or maintained at any time by any ERISA Affiliate, or to which such ERISA Affiliate makes or has made, or has or has had an obligation to make, contributions at any time or with respect to which any ERISA Affiliate has any liability, whether direct or indirect or contingent or otherwise.

"Financial Statements" has the meaning given to such term in (a).

"FLSA" means the United States Fair Labor Standards Act and the rules and regulations promulgated thereunder.

"GAAP" means generally accepted accounting principles as applied in the United States.

"Governmental Entity" means any federal, state or local or foreign government, any political subdivision thereof or any court, administrative or regulatory agency, department, instrumentality, body or commission or other governmental authority or agency, domestic or foreign.

"Hazardous Materials" means any waste, pollutant, contaminant, hazardous substance, toxic, ignitable, reactive or corrosive substance, hazardous waste, special waste, industrial substance, by-product, process-intermediate product or waste, petroleum or petroleum-derived substance or waste, chemical liquids or solids, liquid or gaseous products, or any constituent of any such substance or waste, the use, handling or disposal of which by the Company is in any way governed by or subject to any applicable Law.

"Indemnified Party" has the meaning given to such term in 0.

"Indemnifying Party" has the meaning given to such term in 0.

"Insurance Policy" has the meaning given to such term in 0.

"Intellectual Property" means all intellectual property and other similar proprietary rights in any jurisdiction throughout the world, whether owned or held for use under license, whether registered or unregistered, including such rights in and to: (a) trademarks, trade dress, service marks, certification marks, logos, trade names, corporate names, assumed names and brand names and other indications of origin (collectively, "Trademarks"); (b) patents and patent applications, and any and all divisions, continuations, continuations-in-part, reissues, continuing patent applications, reexaminations, and extensions thereof, any counterparts claiming priority therefrom, utility models, certificates of invention, certificates of registration and like rights (collectively, "Patents"); inventions, invention disclosures, discoveries and improvements, whether or not patentable; (c) writings and other works of authorship, copyright registrations, copyright applications and unregistered common law copyrights, author's rights and photographic releases; (d) trade secrets (including those trade secrets defined in the Uniform Trade Secrets Act and under corresponding foreign Law and common law) and other confidential or non-public business information, including ideas, formulas, compositions, inventions, discoveries and improvements, know-how, manufacturing and production processes and techniques, research and development information, drawings, specifications, designs, plans, proposals, technical data, financial, marketing and business data, pricing and cost information, business and marketing plans and customer and supplier lists and information, in each case whether or not patentable or copyrightable, and rights to limit the use or disclosure thereof by any Person (collectively, "Trade Secrets"); (e) computer software, including programs, source code, object code, algorithms, application programming interfaces, databases and other software-related specifications and documentation (collectively, "Software"); (f) all internet protocol addresses and networks, including domain names, internet e-mail addresses, world wide web (www) and http addresses, network names, network addresses and services (such as mail or website) whether or not used or currently in service and any registrations relating thereto; (g) moral rights and design rights; (h) the goodwill associated with each of the foregoing; (i) all licenses for Intellectual Property for any of the above listed items; and (j) claims, causes of action and defenses relating to the enforcement of any of the foregoing; in each case, including any registrations of, applications to register, and renewals and extensions of, any of the foregoing with or by any Governmental Entity in any jurisdiction. Intellectual Property includes all copies and tangible embodiments of the foregoing (in whatever medium), and any other similar intellectual property rights actually used in connection with the business activities and endeavors of the Company.

"Knowledge" with respect to the Seller means (a) all facts known by each of the directors and officers of the Company after due inquiry and diligence with respect to the matters at hand, and (b) all facts that any of the foregoing individuals should have known with respect to the matters at hand if such individual had made due inquiry and exercised reasonable diligence.

Knowledge is one of the more commonly negotiated definitions in the stock purchase agreement. If the buyer has agreed to allow the seller to qualify certain of its representations and warranties by knowledge, then the scope of the definition of knowledge will directly affect the scope of the qualification and conversely the breadth of the representation and warranty. On the one hand, the seller will attempt to limit the definition of knowledge to the actual knowledge of certain named individuals. The buyer, on the other hand, will take a more expansive position and attempt to include the actual and constructive knowledge of all stockholders, directors, officers, and employees. If the buyer ultimately agrees to a named "knowledge pool," it should attempt to ensure that the individuals identified have knowledge of all functional areas of the target company (human resources, legal, technology, sales, accounting, finance, operations, etc.).

"Labor Laws" means all Laws and all contracts or collective bargaining agreements governing or concerning labor relations, unions and collective bargaining, terms and conditions of employment, employment discrimination, harassment, and retaliation, wages, hours or occupational safety and health, including, the United States Immigration Reform and Control Act of 1986, the United States National Labor Relations Act, the United States Civil Rights Acts of 1866 and 1964, the United States Equal Pay Act, WARN, ERISA, the United States Family and Medical Leave Act, the United States Americans with Disabilities Act, the United States Age Discrimination in Employment Act, the United States Davis Bacon Act, the United States Walsh-Healy Act, the United States Service Contract Act, United States Executive Order

11246, FLSA and the United States Rehabilitation Act of 1973, any state, local or foreign counterparts, and all rules and regulations promulgated under such acts.

"Laws" means all statutes, rules, codes, regulations, restrictions, ordinances, orders, decrees, approvals, directives, judgments, injunctions, writs, awards and decrees of, or issued by, all Governmental Entities.

"Legal Dispute" means any action, suit or proceeding between or among the Parties and their respective Affiliates arising in connection with any disagreement, dispute, controversy or claim arising out of or relating to this Agreement or any related document.

"Liabilities" or "Liability" means debts, liabilities, commitments and obligations (including guarantees and other forms of credit support), whether accrued or fixed, absolute or contingent, matured or unmatured, on- or off-balance sheet, including those arising under any Law or Action and those arising under any Contract or otherwise.

"Licenses" means all notifications, licenses, permits (including environmental, construction and operation permits), franchises, certificates, approvals, exemptions, classifications, registrations and other similar documents and authorizations issued by any Governmental Entity, and applications therefor.

"Liens" mean all mortgages, liens, pledges, security interests, charges, claims, restrictions and encumbrances of any nature whatsoever.

"Loss" means any claim, liability, obligation, loss, cost, Tax, expense, penalty, fine or judgment (at equity or at law, including statutory and common) and damage whenever arising or incurred (including

> **amounts paid in settlement, costs of investigation and reasonable attorneys' fees and expenses).**
>
> **"Material Adverse Effect" means any state of facts, change, event, effect or occurrence that shall have occurred or been threatened (when taken together with all other states of fact, changes, events, effects or occurrences that have occurred or been threatened) that is or could be reasonably likely to be materially adverse to the financial condition, results of operations, properties, assets or liabilities (including contingent liabilities) or prospects of the Company, or the real or personal property of the Company, taken as a whole. A Material Adverse Effect shall also include any state of facts, change, event or occurrence that shall have occurred or been threatened (when taken together with all other states of facts, changes, events, effects or occurrences that have occurred or been threatened) that is or could be reasonably likely to prevent or materially delay the performance by the Company of its obligations under this Agreement or the consummation of any of the Transactions.**

The material adverse effect (MAE) definition has two primary functions in a stock purchase agreement. The first is as a qualification of representations and warranties. The second is as a closing condition in transactions that have a delay between signing and closing. In both cases, the objective of the seller in negotiating the definition of material adverse effect is the same: (1) to remove as much ambiguity as possible; (2) to narrow the definition to events or effects that have actually occurred, thereby eliminating reference to threatened events and "reasonably likely" effects and (3) to focus on market-based measure of material adverse effect (often arguing for a specific dollar threshold). The buyer, on the other hand, will attempt to expand the definition to capture the reality that (1) not all occurrences that are materially adverse to the target company are subject to market-based measures (e.g., prospects); and (2) the definition of MAE should minimally cover future events that are <u>probable or reasonably likely</u>.

The seller will often add carve-out language indicating that some or all of the following will not be considered a material adverse effect (see sample language below): (1) general economic conditions; (2) actions required by the purchase agreement or the public announcement of the transaction; (3) changes in accounting policies and procedures; (4) changes in law; and (5) war, natural disaster, and other acts of God. The buyer should qualify these exceptions with the requirement that they not have a disproportionate impact on the target company as compared to other companies that operate in the target company's industry.

> *provided, however, that "Material Adverse Effect" shall not include any change or effect arising out of or attributable to any of the following, either alone or in combination: (a) changes in general economic conditions or changes or effects that generally affect the [description of] industry or any segment of such industry (including legal and regulatory changes, and changes or effects generally affecting any national, regional or local market for such industry) after the date hereof, unless in the case of the foregoing such change or effect has had or would be reasonably likely to have a materially disproportionate effect with respect to the Company as compared to other Persons in such industries, (b) changes or effects resulting from matters disclosed in any Schedule hereto, (c) changes or effects affecting the financial or securities markets generally after the date hereof, (d) changes or effects arising from the announcement or consummation of the transactions contemplated by this Agreement, or the taking of any action contemplated or permitted by this Agreement, or (e) changes or effects arising or resulting from acts of war (whether or not declared), sabotage, terrorism, military actions or the escalation of any of the foregoing, any hurricane, flood, tornado, earthquake or other natural disaster, or any other force majeure event occurring after the date hereof.*

"Material Contract" and "Material Contracts" have the meanings given to such terms in 0.

"NLRB" means the United States National Labor Relations Board.

"Order" means any order, award, injunction, judgment, decree, ruling, directive, determination, subpoena or verdict or other decision issued by a Governmental Entity.

"Ordinary Course" means, with respect to the Company, the ordinary course of the Company's business consistent with its past practices.

"Organizational Documents" means (a) the certificate of incorporation; (b) articles of incorporation; (c) articles of organization; (d) bylaws; (e) any charter or similar document adopted or filed in connection with the creation, formation or organization of a Person; and (f) any amendment to any of the foregoing.

"Permits" has the meaning given to such term in (a).

"Permitted Liens" means (a) Liens for Taxes not yet due and payable, (b) statutory Liens of landlords, (c) Liens of carriers, warehousemen, mechanics, materialmen and repairmen incurred in the Ordinary Course and not yet delinquent, and (d) in the case of Real Property, zoning, building, or other restrictions, variances, covenants, rights of way, encumbrances, easements and other minor irregularities in title, none of which, individually or in the aggregate, (i) interfere in any material respect with the present use of or occupancy of the affected parcel by the Company, (ii) have more than an immaterial effect on the value thereof or its use, or (iii) would impair the ability of such parcel to be sold for its present use.

"Person" means any individual, corporation, partnership, joint venture, limited liability company, trust, unincorporated organization or Governmental Entity.

"Purchase Price" has the meaning given to such term in 0.

"Receivables" has the meaning given to such term in (a).

"Registered Intellectual Property" means all United States, international and foreign: (a) Patents; (b) Trademarks; (c) registered copyrights and applications for copyright registration; (d) domain name registrations; and (e) any other Intellectual Property that is the subject of an application, certificate, filing, registration or other document issued, filed with, or recorded with any federal, state, local or foreign Governmental Entity or other public body.

"Release" means, with respect to any Hazardous Material, any spilling, leaking, pumping, pouring, emitting, emptying, discharging, injecting, escaping, leaching, dumping or disposing into any surface or ground water, drinking water supply, soil, surface or subsurface strata or medium, or the ambient air.

"Representative" means, with respect to any Person, any director, officer, manager, partner, member, equity holder, agent, employee, attorney, broker, lender, financing source, advisor or other representative of such Person.

"Schedule" has the meaning given to such term in (f).

"Seller Ancillary Document" means any certificate, agreement, document or other instrument, other than this Agreement, to be executed and delivered by a Seller in connection with the Transactions.

"Seller Indemnified Parties" means the Sellers, and their respective heirs, executors, successors and assigns of any of the foregoing.

"Seller Losses" has the meaning given to such term in Section 10.02.

"Suppliers" means any supplier that the Acquired Companies have paid in the aggregate more than $[•] during the twelve (12)-month period ended [_______ __, 20__].

"Surviving Obligations" has the meaning given to such term in (a).

"Surviving Representations" has the meaning given to such term in (a).

"Taxes" means all taxes, assessments, charges, duties, fees, levies and other governmental charges, including income, franchise, capital stock, real property, personal property, tangible, withholding, employment, payroll, social security, social contribution, unemployment compensation, disability, transfer, sales, use, excise, gross receipts, escheat, value-added and all other taxes of any kind for which the Company may have any liability imposed by any Governmental Entity, whether disputed or not, and any charges, interest or penalties imposed by any Governmental Entity.

"Tax Obligations" has the meaning given to such term in (a).

"Tax Representations" has the meaning given to such term in (a).

"Tax Return" means any report, return, declaration or other information required to be supplied to a Governmental Entity in connection with Taxes, including estimated and amended returns.

"Transactions" has the meaning given to such term in the recitals to this Agreement.

"Treasury Regulations" means the Income Tax Regulations promulgated under the Code.

"Unaudited Financial Statements" has the meaning given to such term in (a).

"WARN" means the United States Worker Adjustment and Retraining Notification Act and the rules and regulations promulgated thereunder.

Section 9.02 Construction.

(a) Unless otherwise set forth in this Agreement, all references to Articles, Sections, subsections, Schedules and Exhibits are to Articles, Sections, subsections, Schedules and Exhibits in or to this Agreement.
(b) Unless the context of this Agreement explicitly requires otherwise, (i) references to the plural include the singular, and references to the singular include the plural, (ii) references to any gender include the other genders, (iii) the words "hereof," "herein" and "hereunder" and words of similar import refer to this Agreement as a whole and not to any particular provision of this Agreement, (iv) the words "include," "includes,' and "including" are not limiting and shall be deemed to be followed by the words "without limitation", (v) the terms "day" and "days" mean and refer to calendar days, (vi) the terms "year"

and "years" mean and refer to calendar years, and (vii) all references to "dollars" or "$" means the lawful currency of the United States of America and the settlement of all payments under this Agreement shall be made in such currency.

(c) All accounting terms not specifically defined herein shall be construed in accordance with GAAP.

(d) In the computation of periods of time from a specified date to a later specified date, the word "from" means "from and including"; the words "to" and "until" each mean "to but excluding"; and the word "through" means "to and including."

(e) The Article and Section headings herein are for convenience only and shall not affect the construction hereof.

(f) This Agreement is the result of negotiations among and has been reviewed by each Party's counsel. Accordingly, this Agreement shall not be construed against any Party merely because of such Party's involvement in its preparation.

(g) The disclosure schedules delivered by the Seller to the Buyer immediately prior to the Parties' execution and delivery of this Agreement (each, a "Schedule," and collectively, the "Disclosure Schedules"), are arranged for convenience of reference in Schedules corresponding to the numbered and lettered Sections in this Agreement. Disclosure of any fact or item in any Schedule shall qualify the corresponding Section of this Agreement and shall be deemed to have been disclosed with respect to every other Section of this Agreement only to the extent that such Schedule is cross-referenced in any other Schedule. Capitalized terms used in the Disclosure Schedules and not otherwise defined therein have the meanings given to such terms in this Agreement.

(h) Unless otherwise set forth in this Agreement, references in this Agreement to (i) any document, instrument, contract or agreement (including this Agreement) (A) includes and incorporates all exhibits, schedules and other attachments thereto, (B) includes all documents, instruments, contracts or agreements issued or executed in replacement thereof, and (C) means such document, instrument, contracts or agreement, or replacement or predecessor thereto, as amended, restated, supplemented or otherwise modified from time to time in accordance with its terms and in effect at any given time, and (ii) a particular Law means such Law as amended, modified, supplemented or succeeded, from time to time and in effect at any given time.

[Signature Page Follows]

IN WITNESS WHEREOF, the Parties have caused this Agreement to be duly executed, as of the date first above written.

THE BUYER:

[____________________]
By: ____________________
Name:
Title:

THE SELLER:

[____________________]
By: ____________________
Name:
Title:

Appendix: Sample Stock Purchase Agreement

THIS STOCK PURCHASE AGREEMENT, dated [________ ___, 20__] (the "**Closing Date**"), is made and entered into by and between [Buyer], a Delaware corporation (the "**Buyer**"), and [Seller], a Delaware corporation (the "**Seller**"). The Buyer and the Seller are sometimes referred to individually in this Agreement as a "**Party**" and collectively as the "**Parties.**"

RECITALS

A. [Target Company], a Delaware corporation (the "**Company**"), is engaged in the business of [____________] (the "**Business**").

B. The Seller owns all the Company's issued and outstanding shares of capital stock (the "**Company Shares**").

C. The Parties desire to enter into this Agreement pursuant to which the Seller will sell to the Buyer, and the Buyer will purchase from the Seller, all the Company Shares on the terms and subject to the conditions set forth herein (the "**Acquisition**").

D. Upon the consummation of the transactions contemplated by this Agreement, including the Acquisition (collectively, the "**Transactions**"), the Buyer will own all the Company Shares.

E. The Parties desire to make certain representations, warranties, covenants and other agreements in connection with the foregoing as specified herein.

AGREEMENT

In consideration of the foregoing and the respective representations, warranties, covenants, agreements and conditions set forth in this Agreement, and intending to be legally bound by this Agreement, the Parties agree as follows:

ARTICLE I
THE ACQUISITION; PURCHASE PRICE

Section 1.01 Purchase and Sale. Subject to the terms and conditions of this Agreement, contemporaneously with the execution and delivery of this

Agreement by the Parties, the Seller hereby sells, transfers and delivers to the Buyer, and the Buyer hereby purchases and acquires from the Seller, all the Company Shares, free and clear of all Liens, in exchange for the Buyer's payment of the Purchase Price pursuant to 0.

Section 1.02 Purchase Price. In consideration for the Company Shares, the Buyer shall pay, or cause to be paid, at the Closing, an amount in cash equal to [_______ Dollars ($●)] (the "**Purchase Price**"). After the Closing, the Purchase Price shall be subject to adjustment in accordance with 0.

ARTICLE II

CLOSING; DELIVERIES AND ACTIONS

Section 2.01 Closing. The consummation of the Acquisition (the "**Closing**") shall take place contemporaneously with the execution and delivery of this Agreement by the Parties and shall occur either (a) remotely by the exchange of signature pages hereto and the delivery of those documents described in 0 and 0 by courier, facsimile or e-mail, and the performance of those actions described in 0 and 0, or (b) at such other time and place as the Parties may agree in writing signed by both Parties.

Section 2.02 Seller Closing Deliveries and Contemporaneous Actions. Contemporaneously with the execution and delivery of this Agreement, the Seller shall delivered, or cause to be delivered, to the Buyer the following:

(a) stock certificates representing the Company Shares and accompanying stock powers duly executed by the Seller, evidencing the transfer of the Company Shares to the Buyer;
(b) a certificate of the Secretary or any Assistant Secretary of the Company, dated as of the Closing Date, certifying that: (i) the Company's Organizational Documents, as attached thereto, are true, correct, and complete as of immediately prior to the Closing; (ii) the Company is in good standing in its jurisdiction of formation and in each other jurisdiction where it is qualified to do business, and attached thereto a good standing certificate of the Company, dated no more than thirty (30) days prior to the Closing Date; and (iii) each officer of the Company executing any Company Ancillary Document has been duly elected, has been qualified and, as of the Closing Date, is

an officer of the Company holding the respective offices set opposite his or her name on such certificate and the signature set opposite his or her name thereon is his or her genuine signature;

(c) the Company's organizational record books, minute books and corporate seal; and

(d) a certificate duly completed and executed, dated as of the Closing Date and prepared in accordance with the requirements of U.S. Treasury Regulation sections 1.897-2(h) and 1.1445-2(c)(3), sufficient to establish that an interest in the Company held by a foreign person does not constitute a U.S. real property interest for purposes of Sections 897 and 1445 of the Code.

Section 2.03 <u>Buyer Closing Deliveries and Contemporaneous Actions</u>. Contemporaneous with the execution and delivery of this Agreement, the Buyer shall:

(a) pay, or cause to be paid, to the Seller, the Purchase Price by wire transfer of immediately available funds to an account identified to the Buyer in writing by the Seller no fewer than two (2) Business Days prior to the Closing Date; and

(b) deliver, or cause to be delivered, to the Seller, a certificate of the Secretary or any Assistant Secretary of the Buyer, dated as of the Closing Date, certifying that: (i) the Buyer is in good standing in its jurisdiction of formation and in each other jurisdiction where it is qualified to do business, and attached thereto a good standing certificate of the Buyer, dated no more than thirty (30) days prior to the Closing Date; and (ii) each officer of the Buyer executing any Buyer Ancillary Document has been duly elected, has been qualified and, as of the Closing Date, is an officer of the Buyer holding the respective offices set opposite his or her name on such certificate and the signature set opposite his or her name thereon is his or her genuine signature.

ARTICLE III
SELLER REPRESENTATIONS AND WARRANTIES

The Seller hereby represents and warrants to the Buyer as follows as of the Closing Date:

Section 3.01 Authorization. The Seller has the right, power and capacity to (a) execute and deliver this Agreement and each Seller Ancillary Document, (b) perform the Seller's obligations under this Agreement and each Seller Ancillary Document, and (c) consummate the transactions contemplated this Agreement and each Seller Ancillary Document. The execution and delivery of this Agreement and each Seller Ancillary Document by the Seller, the performance by the Seller of its obligations hereunder and thereunder, and the consummation of the transactions provided for herein and therein, in each case, have been duly and validly authorized by the Seller. This Agreement and each Seller Ancillary Document has been duly executed and delivered by the Seller and each of them constitutes the valid and binding agreement of the Seller, enforceable against the Seller in accordance with their respective terms, subject to applicable bankruptcy, insolvency, reorganization, moratorium or other similar Laws affecting the enforcement of creditors' rights generally, general equitable principles and the discretion of courts in granting equitable remedies.

Section 3.02 Absence of Restrictions and Conflicts. The execution and delivery of this Agreement and the Seller Ancillary Documents, the consummation of the transactions contemplated hereby and thereby and the fulfillment of and compliance with the terms and conditions hereof and thereof do not or will not (as the case may be), with the passing of time or the giving of notice or both, (a) conflict with, result in any breach of, constitute a default (or an event that, with notice or lapse of time or both, would become a default) under, require any approval, consent or authorization of any Person pursuant to, or give to others any rights of termination, acceleration or cancellation of, any Contract, permit, franchise, license or other instrument applicable to the Seller, (b) conflict with or violate any Order to which the Seller is a party or by which the Seller or any of its properties are bound or (c) conflict with or violate any Law applicable to the Seller.

Section 3.03 Ownership of Company Shares.

(a) The Seller has good and valid title to and beneficial ownership of all the Company Shares, and all the Company Shares are (i) validly issued, fully paid, and nonassessable, and (ii) free and clear of all Liens other than restrictions on transfer under state and federal securities Laws.

(b) Other than the Company Shares, the Seller does not own any shares of capital stock or other equity interests in the Company, or any option, warrant, right, call, commitment or right of any kind to have any shares of capital stock or other equity interests in the Company.

Section 3.04 Legal Proceedings. There are no Actions pending or, to the knowledge of the Seller, threatened against, relating to or involving the Seller which could reasonably be expected to adversely affect the Seller's ability to consummate the Transactions or the transactions contemplated by the Seller Ancillary Documents.

Section 3.05 Brokers, Finders and Investment Bankers. The Buyer will not be directly or indirectly obligated to pay or bear (*e.g.*, by virtue of any payment by or obligation of the Seller at or at any time after the Closing) any brokerage, finder's or other fee or commission to any broker, finder or investment banker in connection with the Transactions or any of the transactions contemplated by the Seller Ancillary Documents based on arrangements made by or on behalf of the Seller.

Section 3.06 Amounts Owed to Seller. The Company does not owe and not otherwise obligated to pay the Seller any amount.

ARTICLE IV
COMPANY REPRESENTATIONS AND WARRANTIES

The Sellers represent and warrant to the Buyer as follows as of the Closing Date:

Section 4.01 Organization and Good Standing. The Company is a corporation duly formed and validly existing under the Laws of the State of Delaware and has all requisite power and authority to own, lease and operate its properties and to carry on its business as now being conducted. The Company is duly qualified or registered as a foreign corporation to transact business under the Laws of each jurisdiction where the character of its activities or the location of the properties owned or leased by it requires such qualification or registration. The Seller has heretofore made available to the Buyer true, correct and complete copies of the Company's Organizational Documents as in effect on the Closing Date and the corporate record books with respect to actions taken by its stockholders and board of directors through the Closing Date. Schedule 4.01 contains a true, correct and complete list of the jurisdictions in which the Company is qualified or registered to do business as a foreign corporation.

Section 4.02 Authorization. The Company has the corporate power and authority to (a) execute and deliver each Company Ancillary Document, (b) perform its obligations under each Company Ancillary Document, and (c) consummate the transactions contemplated by each Company Ancillary Document. Each Company Ancillary Document has been duly executed and delivered by the Company, and constitutes the valid and binding agreement of the Company enforceable against the Company in accordance with its respective terms, subject to applicable bankruptcy, insolvency, reorganization, moratorium or other similar Laws affecting the enforcement of creditors' rights generally, general equitable principles and the discretion of courts in granting equitable remedies.

Section 4.03 Capital Stock. The authorized capital stock of the Company consists of [•] shares of common stock, par value $0.01 per share. All the issued and outstanding shares of capital stock of the Company (a) are duly authorized, validly issued, fully paid and nonassessable, (b) are held of record by the Seller, and (c) were not issued in violation of the preemptive rights of any Person or any agreement or Laws. Except as set forth on Schedule 4.03: (A) there are no outstanding options, warrants, rights, calls, commitments, conversion rights, rights of exchange, subscriptions, claims of any character, agreements, obligations, convertible or exchangeable securities or other plans or commitments, contingent or otherwise, relating to the capital stock or other equity interests of the Company, other than as contemplated by this Agreement; (B) there are no outstanding Contracts by which the Company is bound that grants any right to any stockholder of the Company or any other Person to purchase, redeem or otherwise acquire any outstanding shares of capital stock or other equity interests of the Company, or securities or obligations of any kind convertible into any shares of the capital stock or other equity interests of the Company; (C) there are no dividends which have accrued or been declared but are unpaid on the capital stock or other equity interests of the Company; (D) there are no outstanding or authorized stock appreciation, phantom stock, stock plans or similar rights with respect to the Company; and (E) there are no stockholder agreements, voting agreements or other similar agreements relating to the management of the Company by which a stockholder of the Company or the Company is bound. The Company has never purchased, redeemed or otherwise acquired any shares of its capital stock.

Section 4.04 Subsidiaries. The Company does not own, and has never owned (whether directly or indirectly), any capital stock or other equities, securities or interests in any corporation, limited liability company, partnership, trust or other business entity.

Section 4.05 Absence of Restrictions and Conflicts. The execution and delivery of this Agreement, the Seller Ancillary Documents and the Company Ancillary Documents, the consummation of the transactions contemplated hereby and thereby, and the fulfillment of and compliance with the terms and conditions hereof and thereof do not or shall not (as the case may be), with the passing of time or the giving of notice or both, (a) conflict with or violate the Company's Organizational Documents; (b) except as described on Schedule 4.05, conflict with, result in any breach of, constitute a default (or an event that, with notice or lapse of time or both, would become a default) under, require any approval, consent or authorization of any Person pursuant to, or give to others any rights of termination, acceleration or cancellation of, any Material Contract or any other Contract, permit, franchise, license or other instrument applicable to the Company, (iii) conflict with or violate any Order to which the Company is a party or by which the Company or any of its properties are bound, or (iv) conflict with or violate any Law applicable to the Company. No consent, approval, order or authorization of, or registration, declaration or filing with, any Governmental Entity is required with respect to the Company in connection with the execution and delivery of this Agreement, the Seller Ancillary Documents or the Company Ancillary Documents, or the consummation of the transactions contemplated hereby or thereby.

Section 4.06 Real Property.

(a) Schedule 4.06(a) sets forth a true, correct and complete legal description of each parcel of real property owned by the Company (together with all fixtures and improvements thereon) (collectively, the "**Company Owned Real Property**"). The Company has (and will continue to have at the Closing) good and marketable title to each parcel of the Owned Real Property, free and clear of all Liens other than Permitted Liens. [*Alternative*: *The Company does not own, and have never owned, any real property.*]

(b) Schedule 4.06(b) sets forth the true, correct and complete street address of each parcel of real property of which the Company is the lessee (together with all fixtures and improvements thereon) (the "**Company Leased Real Property**" and, together with the Company Owned Real Property, the "**Company Real Property**").

(c) The Company has a valid leasehold interest in the Company Leased Real Property.

(d) No portion of the Company Real Property, or any building or improvement located thereon, violates any Law, including those Laws relating to zoning, building, land use, fire, air, sanitation and noise control. Except for the Permitted Liens, no Company Real Property is subject to (i) any Order or, to the Knowledge of the Seller, threatened or proposed Order, or (ii) any rights of way, building use restrictions, exceptions, variances, reservations or limitations of any nature whatsoever.

(e) The improvements and fixtures on the Company Real Property are in good operating condition and in a state of good maintenance and repair, ordinary wear and tear excepted, are adequate and suitable for the purposes for which they are presently being used. There is no condemnation, expropriation or similar proceeding pending or, to the Knowledge of the Seller, threatened against any of the Company Real Property or any improvement thereon. The Company Real Property constitutes all of the real property utilized by the Acquired Companies in the operation of the Business.

Section 4.07 Title to Assets; Related Matters. The Company has good and marketable title to all of their respective tangible personal property and assets, free and clear of all Liens except Permitted Liens. All equipment and other items of tangible personal property and assets of the Company (a) are in good operating condition and in a state of good maintenance and repair, ordinary wear and tear excepted, (b) are usable in the regular and Ordinary Course, and (c) conform to all applicable Laws. To the Knowledge of the Seller, there is no defect or problem with any of such equipment, tangible personal property or assets, other than ordinary wear and tear. No Person other than the Company owns any equipment or other tangible personal property or assets situated on the Company's premises, except for the leased items that are subject to personal property leases. During the past [__] years, The Company has not sold, transferred or disposed of any assets, other than sales of inventory in the Ordinary Course.

Section 4.08 Financial Statements.

(a) Attached as Schedule 4.08(a) are true, correct and complete copies of (i) the audited balance sheets with respect to the Company as of [________ ___, 20__], [________ ___, 20__] and [________ ___, 20__], and the related audited statements of income, stockholder's equity and cash flows for the fiscal years then ended (collectively, the "**Audited Financial Statements**"), and (ii) the unaudited consolidated balance sheet with respect to the Company as of [________ ___, 20__] (the "**Balance Sheet**") and the related unaudited statement of income, stockholder's equity and cash flows with respect to the Company as of and for the [____]-month period ended [________ ___, 20__] (the "**Unaudited Financial Statements**" and together with the Audited Financial Statements and the Balance Sheet, the "**Financial Statements**"). The Financial Statements have been prepared from, and are in accordance with, the Company's books and records, which books and records accurately reflect the Company's assets and liabilities and are maintained in accordance with GAAP consistently applied throughout the periods indicated, and such books and records have been maintained on a basis consistent with the Company's past practices. The Company maintains adequate internal accounting controls sufficient to provide reasonable assurances regarding the reliability of financial reporting and the preparation of annual financial statements for external purposes in accordance with GAAP. Each balance sheet included in the Financial Statements (including the related notes and schedules) fairly presents the consolidated financial position of the Company as of the date of such balance sheet, and each statement of income, stockholder's equity and cash flows included in the Financial Statements (including the related notes and schedules) fairly presents the consolidated results of operations and changes in cash flows, as the case may be, of the Company or for the periods set forth therein, in each case in accordance with GAAP consistently applied during the periods involved. The Company has not changed any of its accounting (or tax accounting) policies, practices or procedures during the past [__] years.

(b) All accounts receivable reflected on the Balance Sheet that have not been collected (collectively, the "**Receivables**") represent valid obligations of the customers of the Company arising from bona fide transactions entered into in the Ordinary Course, are current and are collectible (net of any reserves set forth on the Balance Sheet) without resort to legal proceedings or collections agencies. The Company has not factored any of the Receivables. During the past [__] years, the Company has collected all accounts receivable in the Ordinary Course.

Section 4.09 No Undisclosed Liabilities. The Company does not have any Liabilities (whether absolute, accrued, contingent or otherwise) that are not adequately reflected or provided for in the Balance Sheet, except Liabilities that have been incurred since the date of the Balance Sheet in the Ordinary Course, and that are not (singly or in the aggregate) material to the Company.

Section 4.10 Absence of Certain Changes.

(a) Since [__________ __, 20__] and except as set forth on Schedule 4.10(a), there has not been (i) any Material Adverse Effect, (ii) any damage, destruction, loss or casualty to property or assets of the Company with a value in excess of $[•] in the aggregate, whether or not covered by insurance, or (iii) any action taken to declare any dividend, pay or set aside for payment any dividend or other distribution, or make any payment to any Company Affiliated Person, other than the payment of salaries in the Ordinary Course or the pre-payment of any indebtedness of the Company.

(b) Since [__________ __, 20__] and except as set forth on Schedule 4.10(b), the Company has:

(i) conduct its businesses in the Ordinary Course and not engage in any new line of business;

(ii) not disposed of or permitted to lapse any right to the use of any Patent, Trademark, trade name, service mark, license or copyright (including any of the Company Intellectual Property), or disposed of or knowingly disclosed to any Person, any trade secret, formula, process, technology or know-how not heretofore a matter of public knowledge;

(iii) not (A) sold any material asset, other than finished goods and inventory sold in the Ordinary Course and obsolete or damaged assets disposed of in the Ordinary Course, (B) created, incurred or assumed any indebtedness secured by any of the Company's assets, (C) granted, created, incurred or suffered to exist any Lien on any of the Company's assets that did not exist on the date of this Agreement, other than Permitted Liens, (D) incurred any material Liability (absolute, accrued or contingent), except in the Ordinary Course, (E) written-off any guaranteed check, note or account receivable, except in the Ordinary Course, (F) write-down the value of any asset or investment on the Company's books or records, except for depreciation and amortization in the Ordinary Course, (G) canceled any debt or waived any material claim or right, or (H) made any legally binding commitment for any capital expenditure to be made on or following the Closing Date;

(iv) not increased in any manner the base compensation of, or entered into any new bonus or incentive agreement or arrangement with, any of its employees, officers, directors or consultants, except in the Ordinary Course;

(v) not paid or agreed to pay any additional pension, retirement allowance or other employee benefit under any Company Benefit Plan to any of its employees or consultants, whether past or present, except in the Ordinary Course;

(vi) not adopted, amended or terminated any Company Benefit Plan or increase the benefits provided under any Company Benefit Plan, or promised or committed to undertake any of the foregoing in the future;

(vii) not amended or terminated any existing Employment Agreement or entered into any new Employment Agreement;

(viii) not made any Tax elections that would affect the Company or the Buyer or change any method or classification of accounting or application of any principles under GAAP; and

(ix) not authorized, or committed or agreed to take, any of the actions described in clauses (ii) through (viii) of this 0(a).

Section 4.11 Legal Proceedings. Except as set forth on Schedule 4.11:

(a) there is no Action pending or, to the Knowledge of the Seller, threatened, either at Law or in equity, against or affecting the Company or any of its properties or assets;
(b) there is no Order issued, promulgated or entered with respect to the Company or any of its properties or assets, in either case, that could adversely affect the operation of the Business; and
(c) there are no Actions of the type described in 0(a) to which the Company, the Seller (in its capacity as an equity owner) or any director, officer or employee of the Company, was a party that have been adjudicated, appealed, withdrawn, dismissed, settled or otherwise resolved during the past [___ (__)] years.

Section 4.12 Compliance with Law; Permits.

(a) The Company is, and has been at all times, in compliance with all applicable Laws in all material respects. The Company has not been charged with, or received written notice that it is under investigation with respect to, and, to the Knowledge of the Seller, is not otherwise now under investigation with respect to, a violation of any applicable Law.
(b) The Company has filed all reports required to be filed with any Governmental Entity and possesses each permit, license, franchise, approval, certificate, consent, waiver, concession, exemption, order, registration, notice, ruling, decision, determination or other authorization of any Governmental Entity necessary for it to own, lease and operate its assets and to carry on its business as currently conducted (each, a "**Permit**"). Schedule 4.12(b) sets forth a true, correct and complete list of the Permits. The Company is in compliance in all material respects with each Permit it possesses and no suspension or cancellation of any Permit is pending or, to the Knowledge of the Seller, threatened. The Company has not received any notice of any Action relating to the revocation or modification of any Permit, and none of the Permits will be subject to suspension, modification, revocation or nonrenewal as a result of the execution and delivery of the this Agreement or the consummation of the Transactions.

Section 4.13 Material Contracts.

(a) Schedule 4.13 sets forth a true, correct and complete list of the following Contracts to which the Company is a party or by which any of its assets or properties is bound (each, a "**Material Contract**" and collectively, the "**Material Contracts**") (other than the Employment Agreements set forth on Schedule 4.15, the Company Benefit Plans set forth on Schedule 4.16(a) and insurance policies on Schedule 4.18):

(i) all bonds, debentures, notes, loans, credit or loan agreements or loan commitments, mortgages, indentures, guarantees or other Contracts relating to the borrowing of money or binding upon any properties or assets (real, personal or mixed, tangible or intangible);
(ii) all leases relating to the Company Real Property or other leases or licenses involving any properties or assets (whether real, personal or mixed, tangible or intangible) involving an annual commitment or payment of more than $[•] individually by the Company;
(iii) all Contracts that limit or restrict the Company or any of its Affiliates or any of its officers or key employees of from engaging in any business in any jurisdiction;
(iv) all Contracts for capital expenditures or the acquisition or construction of fixed assets, which require the Company to pay more than $[•];
(v) all Contracts that grant any Person an increased payment or benefit, or accelerated vesting, upon the execution of this Agreement or the Closing or in connection with the Transactions;
(vi) all Contracts granting any Person a Lien on all or any part of any material asset of the Company;
(vii) all Contracts for the cleanup, abatement or other actions in connection with any Hazardous Materials, the remediation of any existing environmental condition or relating to the performance of any environmental audit or study;
(viii) all Contracts granting to any Person an option or a first refusal, first-offer or similar preferential right to purchase or acquire any asset of the Company;
(ix) all Contracts with any agent, distributor or representative that are not terminable without penalty on advance notice of fewer than thirty (30) days;

(x) all Contracts for the granting or receiving of a license, sublicense or franchise or under which any Person is obligated to pay or has the right to receive a royalty, license fee, franchise fee or similar payment;

(xi) all Contracts (A) with respect to Company-Owned Intellectual Property licensed or transferred to any third party (other than end-user licenses in the Ordinary Course), or (B) pursuant to which a third party has licensed or transferred any Company Intellectual Property to the Company;

(xii) all Contracts providing for the indemnification or holding harmless of any officer, director or employee of the Company or other Person;

(xiii) all Contracts involving (A) the sale or purchase of assets or capital stock (or other equity interests) of any Person (other than inventory in the Ordinary Course), or (B) a merger, consolidation, business combination or similar extraordinary transaction;

(xiv) all joint venture or partnership Contracts and all other Contracts providing for the sharing of any profits;

(xv) all customer Contracts for the provision of goods or services by the Company;

(xvi) all outstanding powers of attorney empowering any Person to act on behalf of the Company; and

(xvii) all existing Contracts and commitments (other than those described in subsections 0 through (xv) of this 00) (A) involving an annual commitment or annual payment to or from the Company of more than $[●] individually or (ii) that is material to the Company or the Business.

(b) The Seller has made available to the Buyer true, correct and complete copies of all Material Contracts. Each Material Contract is legal, valid, binding and enforceable in accordance with its terms with respect to the Company and each other party to such Material Contract. There is no existing material default or breach by the Company under any Material Contract (or event or condition that, with notice or lapse of time or both could constitute a material default or breach), and there is no such material default (or event or condition that, with notice or lapse of time or both, could constitute a material default or breach) with respect to any third party to any

Material Contract. Except as set forth on Schedule 4.13(b), the Company is not participating in any discussions or negotiations regarding modification of, or amendment to, any Material Contract or entry in any new Contract that would constitute a Material Contract. Schedule 4.13(a) identifies with an asterisk each Material Contract set forth therein that requires the consent of, or notice to, the other party thereto to avoid any breach, default or violation of such Contract in connection with the Transactions.

Section 4.14 Tax Returns; Taxes.

(a) All Tax Returns required to have been filed by or with respect to the Company under applicable Laws have been timely filed, and each such Tax Return was correct and complete in all material respects and was prepared in substantial compliance with all applicable Laws. All Taxes due and owing by or with respect to the Company (whether or not shown as due on any Tax Return) have been paid. The Company is not the beneficiary of any extension of time within which to file any Tax Return. No claim has ever been made or, to the Knowledge of the Seller, threatened by a Governmental Entity in a jurisdiction where the Company does not file Tax Returns that the Company is or may be subject to taxation by that jurisdiction.

(b) The Company has not received from any Governmental Entity (including in jurisdictions where the Company has not filed any Tax Return) any (i) written or, to the Knowledge of the Seller, oral notice indicating an intent to open an audit or other review, (ii) request for information related to Tax matters, or (iii) notice of deficiency or proposed adjustment for any amount of Tax proposed, asserted, or assessed by any Governmental Entity against the Company. Schedule 4.14(b) lists all federal, state, local and foreign income and sales and use Tax Returns filed with respect to the Company for taxable periods ended on or after [__________ __, 20__], indicates which of such Tax Returns have been audited, and indicates which of such Tax Returns currently are the subject of audit. The Seller has delivered or otherwise made available to the Buyer true, correct and complete copies of all federal income Tax Returns that include the income of the Company, examination reports that may affect the Tax liability attributable to the Company, and statements of deficiencies assessed against or agreed to by the Company for taxable periods beginning on or after [__________, 20__].

(c) There are no Liens for Taxes (other than Taxes not yet due and payable) upon any of the Company's assets.

(d) The Company has withheld and paid all Taxes required to have been withheld and paid in connection with amounts paid or owing to any employee, independent contractor, creditor, stockholder, or other third party.

(e) The Company has not waived any statute of limitations in respect of Taxes or agreed to any extension of time with respect to a Tax assessment or deficiency.

(f) The Company is not a party to any Contract or other arrangement that has resulted or would result, separately or in the aggregate, in the payment of any "excess parachute payment" within the meaning of Section 280G of the Code (or any corresponding provision of state, local or foreign Tax Law).

Section 4.15 Company Benefit Plans.

(a) Schedule 4.15(a) contains a true, correct and complete list of the Company Benefit Plans and any special tax status enjoyed by such Company Benefit Plan is noted on Schedule 4.15(a).

(b) Except as set forth on Schedule 4.15(b):

   (i) The Company's records accurately reflect the employment or service histories of each of their respective employees, independent contractors, contingent workers and leased employees, including their hours of service, and all such records are maintained in a usable form.

   (ii) No Company Benefit Plan or ERISA Affiliate Plan is or was subject to Title IV of ERISA or Section 412 of the Code, and no Company Benefit Plan or ERISA Affiliate Plan is or was a "multiemployer pension plan" (as defined in Section 3(37) of ERISA) or subject to Section 302 of ERISA. The Company has not terminated or withdrawn from or sought a funding waiver with respect to, and no fact exists that could reasonably be expected to result in a termination or withdrawal from or seeking a funding waiver with respect to, the Company Benefit Plan that is subject to Title IV of ERISA. The Company has not incurred, and no fact exists that reasonably could be expected to result in, liability to the Company as a result of a termination, withdrawal or funding waiver with respect to an ERISA Affiliate Plan.

(iii) No Company Benefit Plan or ERISA Affiliate Plan is or was a "multiple employer welfare arrangement" (as defined in Section 3(40) of ERISA).

(iv) Each Company Benefit Plan has been established, registered, qualified, invested, operated and administered in all respects in accordance with its terms and in compliance with ERISA, the Code and all Applicable Benefit Laws. The Company has not incurred, and no fact exists that reasonably could be expected to result in any liability to the Company with respect to any Company Benefit Plan or any ERISA Affiliate Plan, including any liability, tax, penalty or fee under ERISA, the Code or any Applicable Benefit Law (other than to pay premiums, contributions or benefits in the Ordinary Course).

(v) No fact or circumstance exists that could adversely affect the tax-exempt status of a Company Benefit Plan that is intended to be tax-exempt. Further, each Company Benefit Plan intended to be "qualified" within the meaning of Section 401(a) of the Code and the trusts maintained thereunder that are intended to be exempt from taxation under Section 501(a) of the Code has received a favorable determination or other letter indicating that it is so qualified based on the terms of the plan or plans as currently in effect, and all amendments required to be adopted on or before the date of this Agreement have been timely and properly adopted.

(vi) No insurance policy or any other Contract affecting any Company Benefit Plan requires or permits a retroactive increase in premiums or payments due thereunder. The level of insurance reserves under each insured Company Benefit Plan is reasonable and sufficient to provide for all incurred but unreported claims.

(vii) The execution and delivery of this Agreement and the consummation of the Transactions will not (A) entitle any current or former employee, director, officer, consultant, independent contractors, contingent worker or leased employee (or any of their dependents, spouses or beneficiaries) of the Company to severance pay, unemployment compensation or any other payment, or (B) accelerate the time of payment or vesting, or increase the amount of compensation due any such individual.

(viii) No Company Benefit Plan provides for post-retirement medical or other welfare benefits other than the medical benefits required to be provided under Part 6 of Subtitle B of Title I of ERISA.

(ix) No Company Benefit Plan provides benefits which are subject to taxation under Section 409A of the Code.

Section 4.16 Labor and Employment Matters.

(a) Schedule 4.16(a) sets forth a true, correct and complete list of (i) all employees (whether active, on leave, full-time, part-time or otherwise) of the Company, including all officers of the Company (collectively, the "**Employees**"); (ii) all current paid consultants, dependent contractors or independent contractors engaged by the Company (collectively, the "**Consultants**"); and (iii) all retirees and terminated employees for which the Company has any benefits responsibility or other continuing or contingent obligation; together, in each case, with the following for each such Person, such Person's: (A) current rate of compensation or fees; (B) date of hire; (C) age; (D) title and/or job description; (E) part-time or full-time status; (F) accrued and unused vacation days; (G) accrued and unused sick days; (H) if on leave, the category and status of such leave (including expected return date); (I) location of employment; (J) the terms on which each of the Consultants are engaged; (K) employee benefit coverage selected; and (L) status as exempt or nonexempt from overtime under the FLSA (for only those Employees employed by the Company in the United States). Except as indicated on Schedule 4.16(a), all officers and employees of the Company are active.

(b) Except as set forth on Schedule 4.16(b), the Company is not a party to, or otherwise bound by, any Employment Agreement. The Seller has made available to the Buyer true, correct and complete copies of each Employment Agreement set forth on Schedule 4.16(b). Each such Employment Agreement is legal, valid and binding of the

Company and enforceable against the Company in accordance with its terms. There is no existing default or breach by the Company under any Employment Agreement to which it is a party (or event or condition that, with notice or lapse of time or both could constitute a default or breach thereunder) and there is no such default, or event or condition that, with notice or lapse of time or both, could constitute a default or breach) with respect to any third party to any Employment Agreement to which the Company is a party.

(c) The Company has not received a claim from any Governmental Entity to the effect that the Company has (i) improperly classified as an independent contractor any officer or employee of the Company or (ii) improperly classified an employee as "exempt" or "non-exempt" under the FLSA or any state, local or foreign counterpart.

(d) Except as set forth on Schedule 4.16(d): (i) the Company is not a party to any collective bargaining agreement, contract or legally binding commitment to any trade union or employee organization or group in respect of or affecting employees; (ii) the Company is not engaged in any negotiation with any trade union or employee organization; (iii) the Company has not engaged in any unfair labor practice within the meaning of the NLRB, and there is no pending or, to the Knowledge of the Seller, threatened complaint regarding any alleged unfair labor practices as so defined; (iv) there is no strike, labor dispute, work slow down or stoppage pending or, to the Knowledge of the Seller, threatened against the Company; (v) there is no grievance or arbitration proceeding arising out of or under any collective bargaining agreement which is pending or, to the Knowledge of the Seller, threatened against the Company; (vi) the Company has not experienced any material work stoppage; (vii) the Company is not the subject of any union organization effort; and (viii) the Company is (and has been) in compliance with all applicable Labor Laws.

Section 4.17 Insurance Policies. Schedule 4.17 sets forth a true, correct and complete list of all policies of insurance carried by or for the benefit of the Company during the [___ (__)]-year period ended on the date hereof (each, an "**Insurance Policy**"), specifying the insurer, the amount of and nature of coverage, the policy limits or amounts of coverage, the deductible amount (if any), the annual premiums with respect thereto, and the date through which coverage will continue by virtue of premiums already paid. Each Insurance Policy (a) is in full force and effect, (b) is valid and binding in accordance with its terms, and (c) will continue in effect after the Closing Date. During the past [___ (__)] years, there has been maintained for the benefit of the Company insurance coverage that is substantially similar to the coverage set forth in the Insurance Policies. The Company has not (i) received notice of any cancellation or non-renewal or threat of cancellation or non-renewal of any Insurance Policy, (ii) reached or exceeded its policy limits for any Insurance Policy, (iii) failed to give any notice of any claim under any Insurance Policy in due and timely fashion, or (iv) been denied or turned down for coverage under any Insurance Policy.

Section 4.18 Environmental, Health and Safety Matters. Except as set forth on Schedule 4.18:

(a) the Company possess all Permits and approvals required under, and are in compliance in all material respects with, all Environmental Laws, and the Company is in compliance in all material respects with all applicable limitations, restrictions, conditions, standards, prohibitions, requirements, obligations, schedules and timetables contained in all Environmental Laws or contained in any other Law, or any notice or demand letter issued thereunder;

(b) the Company has not received notice of actual or threatened liability under CERCLA or any similar foreign, state or local Law from any Governmental Entity or any third party, and there is no fact or circumstance that could form the basis for the assertion of any claim against the Company under any Environmental Law, including CERCLA or any similar local, state or foreign Law with respect to any on-site or off-site location;

(c) the Company is not subject to any Loss, contingent or otherwise, incurred or imposed or based upon any provision of any Environmental Law or arising out of (i) any act or omission of the Company, or an employee, agent or representative of the Company or (ii) the ownership, use, control or operation by the Company of any facility, site, area or property (including any facility, site, area or property currently or previously owned or leased by the Company) from which any Hazardous Material was Released; and

(d) the Seller has made available to the Buyer true, correct and complete copies of all reports, correspondence, memoranda, computer data and the complete files relating to the Company's environmental matters; and the Company has not paid any fine, penalty or assessment during the past [____ (__)] years with respect to environmental matters.

Section 4.19 Intellectual Property.

(a) Schedule 4.20(a) sets forth a true, correct and complete listing of all Company Registered Intellectual Property, which identifies that which is owned and that which is licensed by the Company.

(b) No Company Intellectual Property or product or service used by the Company related to Company Intellectual Property is subject to any Action or Order (i) restricting in any manner the use, transfer or licensing thereof by the Company, or (ii) that may affect the validity, use or enforceability of the Company Intellectual Property or any such product or service. Each item of Company Registered Intellectual Property is valid and subsisting. All necessary registration, maintenance and renewal fees currently due or due within the next twenty (20) days in connection with Company Registered Intellectual Property have been made and all necessary documents, recordations and certifications in connection with the Company Registered Intellectual Property have been filed with the relevant patent, copyright, trademark or other authorities in the United States or foreign jurisdictions, as the case may be, for the purpose of maintaining such Company Registered Intellectual Property.

(c) The Company owns and has good and exclusive title to, or has licenses sufficient for the conduct of the Business as currently conducted and as proposed to be conducted to, each item of Company Intellectual Property, free and clear of any Lien, excluding licenses and related restrictions. The Company is the exclusive owner or exclusive licensee of the trademarks and service marks, trade names and domain names used by the Company, including the sale of any products or the provision of any services of the Company, free and clear of all Liens.

(d) The Company owns exclusively and has good title to all copyrighted works used by the Company that (i) are products of the Company, or

(ii) the Company otherwise expressly purports to own, free and clear of all Liens. Schedule 4.20(d) lists all works of original authorship used by the Company and prepared by or on behalf of the Company (including software programs) by title, version number, author(s) and publication date, if any, regardless of whether the Company has obtained or is seeking a copyright registration for such works.

(e) To the extent that the Company Intellectual Property has been developed or created by a third party for the Company, the Company has a written Contract with such third party with respect thereto and the Company thereby either (i) has obtained ownership of and is the exclusive owner of, or (ii) has obtained a license sufficient for the operations of the Business as currently conducted and as proposed to be conducted to, all of such third party's Intellectual Property in such work, material or invention by operation of law or by valid assignment.

(f) The operations of the Business as currently conducted and as proposed to be conducted, including the Company's design, development, marketing and sale of the products or services of the Company, including with respect to products currently under development, has not and does not infringe, violate or misappropriate in any manner the Intellectual Property of any third party or constitute unfair competition or trade practices under the Laws of any jurisdiction.

(g) The Company has not received written notice, and to the Knowledge of the Seller, there is no other overt threat, from any third party, that the operation of the Business as it is currently conducted and as proposed to be conducted, or any act, product or service of the Company, infringes, violates or misappropriates the Intellectual Property of any third party or constitutes unfair competition or trade practices under the Laws of any jurisdiction.

(h) To the Knowledge of the Seller, no Person has infringed, violated or misappropriated or is infringing, violating or misappropriating any Company Intellectual Property.

(i) The Company has taken reasonable steps to protect their rights in the Confidential Information and any trade secret or confidential information of third parties used by any Acquired Company, and, without limiting the generality of the foregoing, the Company has enforced a policy requiring each employee and contractor to execute a proprietary information/confidentiality agreement in substantially the form provided to the Buyer, and, except under confidentiality obligations to which the receiving parties are bound, the Company has disclosed any Confidential Information or any such trade secret or confidential information of third parties.

Section 4.20 Software.

(a) Schedule 4.20(a) sets forth a true, correct and complete list of (i) the Company Proprietary Software, (ii) the Company Licensed Software, and (iii) all technical and restricted materials relating to the acquisition, design, development, use or maintenance of computer code program documentation and materials used by the Company.

(b) The Company has all right, title and interest in and to all Intellectual Property rights in the Company Proprietary Software. The Company has developed the Company Proprietary Software through its own efforts, and for its own account, and the Company Proprietary Software is free and clear of all Liens other than Permitted Liens. The use of the Company Software does not breach any material term of any license or other Contract between the Company and any third party. The Company is in compliance with the terms and conditions of all license agreements in favor of the Company relating to the Company Licensed Software.

(c) To the Knowledge of the Seller, the Company Proprietary Software does not infringe any patent, copyright or trade secret or any other Intellectual Property right of any third party. The source code for the Company Proprietary Software has been maintained in confidence.

(d) The Company Proprietary Software was: (i) developed by the Company's employees working within the scope of their employment at the time of such development; (ii) developed by agents, consultants, contractors or other Persons who have executed appropriate instruments of assignment in favor of the Company as assignee that have conveyed to the Company ownership of all of its Intellectual Property rights in the Company Proprietary Software; or (iii) acquired by the Company in connection with acquisitions in which the Company obtained appropriate representations, warranties and indemnities from the transferring party relating to the title to the Company Proprietary Software. The Company has not received notice from any third party claiming any right, title or interest in the Company Proprietary Software.

(e) The Company has not granted rights in the Company Software to any third party.

Section 4.21 Transactions with Affiliates. Except as set forth Schedule 4.21, no Company Affiliated Person has any interest in: (a) any Contract with, or relating to, the Company or its properties or assets; (b) any loan, arrangement, understanding or Contract for or relating to the Company or its properties or assets; or (c) any property (real, personal or mixed), tangible or intangible, used by any the Company. Schedule 4.21 also sets forth a true, correct and complete list of all accounts receivable, notes receivable and other receivables and accounts payable owed to or due from any Affiliate of the Company to or from the Company.

Section 4.22 Undisclosed Payments. Neither the Company nor any of its or directors, nor anyone acting on behalf of any of them, has made or received any payment not correctly categorized and fully disclosed in the Company's books and records in connection with or in any way relating to or affecting the Company.

Section 4.23 Customer and Supplier Relations.

(a) Schedule 4.23(a) sets forth a true, correct and complete list of the names and addresses of the Customers, and the amount of sales to each Customer during the twelve (12)-month period ending [________ __, 20__]. The Company maintain good relations with the Customers and, to the Knowledge of the Seller, no event has occurred that could adversely affect the Company's relations with any Customer in any material respect. Except as set forth in Schedule 4.23(a), no Customer during the prior twelve (12) months has canceled, terminated or made any threat to cancel or otherwise terminate any of such Customer's relations with the Company or to decrease in any material amount such Customer's usage of the Company's services or products. No Customer has notified the Company that such Customer will terminate or materially alter its business relations with the Company, either as a result of the Transactions or otherwise.

(b) Schedule 4.23(b) sets forth a true, correct and complete list of the names and addresses of the Suppliers, and the annualized amount of purchases from each Supplier during the twelve (12)-month period ending [_______ __, 20__]. The Company maintain good relations with the Suppliers and, to the Knowledge of the Seller, no event has occurred that could adversely affect the Company's relations with any Supplier in any material respect. Except as set forth on Schedule 4.23(b), no Supplier (or former Supplier) during the prior twelve (12) months has canceled, terminated or, to the Knowledge of the Seller, made any threat to cancel or otherwise terminate any of its Contracts or commitments with the Company or to decrease its supply of any services or products. No Supplier has notified the Company that such Supplier will terminate or materially alter such Supplier's business relations with any of the Company, either as a result of the Transactions or otherwise.

Section 4.24 Brokers, Finders and Investment Bankers. The Buyer will not be directly or indirectly obligated to pay or bear (*e.g.*, by virtue of any payment by or obligation of the Company at or at any time after the Closing) any brokerage, finder's or other fee or commission to any broker, finder or investment banker in connection with the Transactions or any of the transactions contemplated by the Company Ancillary Documents or Seller Ancillary Documents based on arrangements made by or on behalf of the Company, except as specifically provided herein.

Section 4.25 Disclosure. None of the information supplied by or on behalf of the Company to the Buyer, and no representation, warranty or covenant made by the Seller in this Agreement or any Seller Ancillary Document or by the Company in any Company Ancillary Document contains an untrue statement of a material fact or omits to state a material fact required to be stated herein or therein or necessary to make the statements contained herein or therein not misleading. The financial projections relating to the Company delivered to the Buyer are made in good faith and are based upon reasonable assumptions, and the Seller is not aware of any fact or set of circumstances that could lead the Buyer to believe that such projections are incorrect or misleading in any material respect.

ARTICLE V
REPRESENTATIONS AND WARRANTIES OF THE BUYER

The Buyer hereby represents and warrants to the Seller as follows as of the Closing Date:

Section 5.01 Organization. The Buyer is a corporation duly organized, validly existing and in good standing under the Laws of the State of Delaware and has all requisite corporate power and authority to own, lease and operate its properties and to carry on its business as now being conducted.

Section 5.02 Authorization. The Buyer has full power and authority to (a) execute and deliver this Agreement and each Buyer Ancillary Document, (b) perform its obligations under this Agreement and each Buyer Ancillary Document, and (c) consummate the transactions contemplated by this Agreement and each Buyer Ancillary Document. This Agreement and each Buyer Ancillary Document has been duly executed and delivered by the Buyer, and each of them constitutes the valid and binding agreement of the Buyer, enforceable against the Buyer in accordance with their respective terms, subject to applicable bankruptcy, insolvency, reorganization, moratorium or other similar Laws affecting the enforcement of creditors' rights generally, general equitable principles and the discretion of courts in granting equitable remedies.

Section 5.03 Absence of Restrictions and Conflicts. The execution and delivery of this Agreement and the Buyer Ancillary Documents, the consummation of the transactions contemplated hereby and thereby and the fulfillment of, and compliance with, the terms and conditions hereof and thereof do not or shall not, as the case may be, with the passing of time or the giving of notice or both, violate or conflict with, constitute a breach of or default under, result in the loss of any benefit under, or permit the acceleration of any obligation under, (a) any term or provision of the Buyer's Organizational Documents, (b) any Contract to which the Buyer is a party, (c) any Order to which the Buyer is a party or by which the Buyer or any of its properties is bound, or (d) any Law applicable to the Buyer.

Section 5.04 Brokers, Finders and Investment Bankers. None of the Sellers will be directly or indirectly obligated to pay or bear (*e.g.*, by virtue of any payment by or obligation of the Buyer at or at any time after the Closing) any brokerage, finder's or other fee or commission to any broker, finder or investment banker in connection with the Transactions or any of the transactions contemplated by the Buyer Ancillary Documents based on arrangements made by or on behalf of the Buyer.

ARTICLE VI
CERTAIN COVENANTS AND AGREEMENTS

Section 6.01 Public Announcements. Neither Party shall make any public announcements regarding this Agreement or the Transactions, including any announcements to the financial community, any Governmental Entity, any employees of the Company, any customers or suppliers of the Company or the general public, without the prior written consent of the other Party; provided, however, that the foregoing prohibition shall not apply to any announcement that is required by Law, in which case the Party required to make such announcement shall use its commercially reasonable efforts to deliver to the other Party a copy of the same before such announcement is made.

Section 6.02 Seller Release. In consideration for the agreement and covenants of the Buyer set forth in this Agreement, the Seller, on its own behalf, and on behalf of each of its Affiliates, hereby knowingly, voluntarily and unconditionally releases and forever discharges from and for, and covenants not to sue the Buyer, the Company, or any predecessor, successor, parent, subsidiary or other Affiliate of the Buyer or the Company, or any of their respective current and former officers, directors, employees, agents, or representatives for or with respect to, any and all claims, causes of action, demands, suits, debts, obligations, liabilities, damages, losses, costs, and expenses (including attorneys' fees) of every kind or nature whatsoever, known or unknown, actual or potential, suspected or unsuspected, fixed or contingent, that the Seller has or may have, now or in the future, arising out of, relating to, or resulting from any act of commission or omission, errors, negligence, strict liability, breach of contract, tort, violations of law, matter or cause whatsoever from the beginning of time to the Closing Date; provided, however, that such release shall not cover: (a) any claims against the Buyer or any of its Affiliates (other than the Company) unrelated in any way to the Company or (b) any claims against the Buyer arising under this Agreement, any Seller Ancillary Document or any Buyer Ancillary Document.

Section 6.03 Cooperation Following the Closing. Following the Closing, each Party shall deliver to the other Party such further information and documents and shall execute and deliver to the other Party such further instruments and agreements as such other Party reasonably requests to consummate or confirm the Transactions, to accomplish the purpose of this Agreement or to assure to such other Party the benefits of this Agreement.

Section 6.04 Non-Competition.

(a) The Stockholders hereby acknowledge that (A) the Company currently conducts, has plans to conduct or previously has conducted Business Activities (as defined below) throughout the Territory and (B) to adequately protect the interest of Purchaser in the Company, it is essential that any non-compete covenant with respect thereto cover all of the Business Activities and the entire Territory and (C) part of the Purchase Price was allocated as to compensate the noncompetition obligations of Stockholders. "Business Activities" means any line of business throughout the Territory which the Company (1) is presently engaged on the Closing Date, (2) was previously engaged in the five (5) year period preceding the Closing Date, or (3) as of the Closing Date, has written plans to enter. So there may be no doubt, Business Activities shall include, without limitation, any kind of activities that are directly or indirectly, related to (v) credit reporting, business reporting, (w) personal information solutions, (x) credit data marketing services, (y) identification management and (z) analytics and the development of solutions, as such relates to any of the foregoing. "Territory" shall mean the States of Georgia, Florida, Alabama, North Carolina and South Carolina.

(b) During the five (5) year period following the Closing Date (the "Non-compete Period"), neither the Stockholders, nor any of their respective Affiliates or representatives (acting on their behalf), shall in any manner directly or indirectly, conduct Business Activities or offer products or services competitive therewith in the Territory or otherwise engage in, have an equity or profit interest in, or render services (of an executive, marketing, manufacturing, research and development, administrative, financial, or consulting nature) to any Person that conducts any of the Business Activities or offers products or services competitive therewith in the Territory.

ARTICLE VII
INDEMNIFICATION

Section 7.01 Indemnification Obligations of the Seller. The Seller shall indemnify, defend and hold harmless the Buyer Indemnified Parties from, against, and in respect of, any and all Losses arising out of or relating to:

(a) any breach of or inaccuracy in any representation or warranty made by the Seller in 0 or 0 of this Agreement, any Seller Ancillary Document or any Company Ancillary Document;
(b) any claim asserted or held by any Person (against any Buyer Indemnified Party) that, if meritorious, would constitute or give rise to a breach of or inaccuracy in any representation or warranty made by the Seller in 0 or 0 of this Agreement, any Seller Ancillary Document or any Company Ancillary Document;
(c) any breach by the Seller of any covenant, agreement or undertaking made by the Seller in this Agreement, any Seller Ancillary Document or any Company Ancillary Document;
(d) any liability or obligation relating to claims by any Person relating to any equity interest in the Company or purported equity interest in the Company granted prior to the Closing Date; or
(e) any liability of any of the Company (i) for any Taxes of the Company with respect to any Tax period or portion thereof ending on or before the Closing Date (or for any Tax period beginning before and ending after the Closing Date to the extent allocable to the portion of such period beginning before and ending on the Closing Date), and (ii) for the unpaid Taxes of any Person (other than the Company) under Treasury Regulations section 1.1502-6 (or any similar provision of state, local, or foreign law), as a transferee of successor, by contract, or otherwise.

The Losses of the Buyer Indemnified Parties described in this 0 as to which the Buyer Indemnified Parties are entitled to indemnification are collectively referred to as "**Buyer Losses**".

Section 7.02 Indemnification Obligations of the Buyer. The Buyer shall indemnify and hold harmless the Seller Indemnified Parties from, against and in respect of any and all Losses arising out of or relating to:

(a) any breach or inaccuracy of any representation or warranty made by the Buyer in 0 of this Agreement or any Buyer Ancillary Document; or
(b) any breach of any covenant, agreement or undertaking made by the Buyer in this Agreement or any Buyer Ancillary Document.

The Losses of the Seller Indemnified Parties described in this 0 as to which the Seller Indemnified Parties are entitled to indemnification are collectively referred to as "**Seller Losses**".

Section 7.03 Indemnification Procedure.

(a) A Buyer Indemnified Party or a Seller Indemnified Party, as the case may be (an "**Indemnified Party**") shall notify promptly the Buyer or the Seller, as the case may be (the "**Indemnifying Party**"), following such Indemnified Party's receipt of notice from a third party, including any Governmental Entity, of any Action (a "**Third Party Claim**") with respect to which such Indemnified Party may be entitled to receive payment from the Indemnifying Party for any Buyer Loss or any Seller Loss, as the case may be; provided, however, that an Indemnified Party's failure to so notify the Indemnifying Party will relieve the Indemnifying Party from liability under this Agreement with respect to such Third Party Claim only if, and only to the extent that, such failure to so notify the Indemnifying Party results in the forfeiture by the Indemnifying Party of rights and defenses that would have otherwise been available to the Indemnifying Party with respect to such Third Party Claim. The Indemnified Party's notice shall describe the Third Party Claim in reasonable detail to the extent practicable based upon the facts then known by the Indemnified Party, and shall indicate the amount (estimated, if necessary) of the Loss that has been or may be suffered. The Indemnifying Party shall have the right, upon (i) delivering written notice to the Indemnified Party within fifteen (15) days after receiving notice of such Third Party Claim and (ii) assuming full responsibility for any Buyer Losses or Seller Losses, as the case may be, resulting from such Third Party Claim, to assume the defense of such Third Party Claim, including the employment of counsel reasonably satisfactory to the Indemnified Party and the payment of the fees and disbursements of such counsel. Notwithstanding the foregoing, the Indemnifying Party shall not have any right to assume the defense of any Third Party Claims if (x) such Third Party Claim relates to any Company Intellectual Property or any Governmental Entity, (y) such Third Party Claim seeks a finding of criminal liability of, equitable remedies against, or any judgment or term that in any manner affects, restrains or interferes with the business of, the Indemnified Party or any of the Indemnified Party's Affiliates, or (z) the Indemnified Party reasonably believes that the interests of the Indemnifying Party and the Indemnified Party with respect to the such Third Party Claim are in conflict with one another, and as a result, the Indemnifying Party could not adequately represent the interests of the Indemnified Party in such Third Party Claim. If, however, the Indemnifying Party declines or fails to assume the defense of the Third Party Claim on the terms provided in the immediately preceding sentence or to employ counsel reasonably satisfactory to the Indemnified Party, in either case within such fifteen (15)-day period, then the Indemnifying Party shall pay the reasonable fees and disbursements of counsel for the Indemnified Party as incurred. In any Third Party Claim for which indemnification is being sought under this Agreement, the Indemnified Party or the Indemnifying Party, whichever is not assuming the defense of such Third Party Claim, shall have the right to participate in such matter and to retain its own counsel at such Party's own expense. The Indemnifying Party or the Indemnified Party, as the case may be, shall at all times use reasonable efforts to keep the Indemnifying Party or Indemnified Party, as the case may be, reasonably apprised of the status of the defense of any matter the defense of which it is maintaining and to cooperate in good faith with each other with respect to the defense of any such matter, which cooperation shall include furnishing or causing to be furnished such records, information, and testimony (subject to any applicable confidentiality agreement), and attending such conferences, discovery proceedings, hearings, trials, or appeals as may be reasonably requested in connection therewith; provided, however, that neither the Indemnified Party nor the Indemnifying Party will be required to grant access to or furnish information to the other party or such other party's Representatives to the extent that such access or the furnishing of such information would result in the waiver of an attorney-client or attorney work product privilege; provided, that, in each such case, the Indemnifying Party or the Indemnified Party, as the case may be, shall identify to the other party in reasonable detail such withheld information and the basis for such non disclosure.

(b) An Indemnified Party shall not settle or compromise any Third Party Claim or consent to the entry of any judgment with respect to any Third Party Claim, in each case, for which indemnification is being sought under this Agreement, without the prior written consent of the Indemnifying Party (not to be unreasonably withheld, conditioned or delayed), unless (i) the Indemnifying Party fails to assume and maintain the defense of such Third Party Claim pursuant to 00, or (ii) such settlement, compromise or consent includes an unconditional release of the Indemnifying Party and its officers, directors, employees and Affiliates from all liability arising out of such Third Party Claim. An Indemnifying Party shall not, without the prior written consent of the Indemnified Party (not to be unreasonably withheld, conditioned or delayed), settle or compromise any Third Party Claim or consent to the entry of any judgment with respect to any Third Party Claim, in each case, for which indemnification is being sought under this Agreement, unless (x) such settlement, compromise or consent includes an unconditional release of the Indemnified Party and its officers, directors, employees and Affiliates from all liability arising out of such Third Party Claim, (y) does not contain any admission or statement suggesting any wrongdoing or liability on behalf of the Indemnified Party, and (z) does not contain any equitable order, judgment or term that in any manner affects, restrains or interferes with the business of the Indemnified Party or any of the Indemnified Party's Affiliates.

(c) If an Indemnified Party claims a right to payment pursuant to this 0, such Indemnified Party shall send written notice of such claim to the appropriate Indemnifying Party. Such notice shall specify the basis for such claim. The failure by any Indemnified Party so to notify the Indemnifying Party shall not relieve the Indemnifying Party from any liability that it may have to such Indemnified Party with respect to any claim made pursuant to this 0, it being understood that notices for claims in respect of a breach of a representation or warranty must be delivered prior to the expiration of the Claims Period under 0. If the Indemnifying Party does not notify the Indemnified Party that the Indemnifying Party disputes its liability to the Indemnified Party under this 0 or the amount thereof within thirty (30) days after it receives such notice, then the claim specified by the Indemnified Party in such notice shall be conclusively deemed a liability of the Indemnifying Party under this 0, and the Indemnifying Party shall pay the amount of such liability to the Indemnified Party on demand or, in the case of any notice in which the amount of the claim (or any portion of the claim) is estimated, on such later date when the amount of such claim (or such portion of such claim) becomes finally determined. If the Indemnifying Party has timely disputed its liability with respect to such claim as provided above, as promptly as possible, such Indemnified Party and the appropriate Indemnifying Party shall establish the merits and amount of such claim (by mutual agreement, litigation, arbitration or otherwise) and, within five (5) Business Days after the final determination of the merits and amount of such claim, the Indemnifying Party shall pay to the Indemnified Party immediately available funds in an amount equal to such claim as determined under this Agreement.

Section 7.04 Claims Period. The Claims Periods under this Agreement shall begin on the date of this Agreement and terminate as follows:

(a) with respect to Buyer Losses arising under (i) 0 or (a) with respect to any breach or inaccuracy of any representation or warranty in 0 (Authorization), 0 (Ownership of Company Shares), 0 (Brokers, Finders and Investment Bankers), and 0 (Amounts Owed to Sellers), 0 (Organization), 0 (Authorization), 0 (Capital Stock), 0 (Transactions with Affiliates), and 0 (Brokers, Finders and Investment Bankers) (collectively, the "**Surviving Representations**"), or (ii) (b), (collectively, the "**Surviving Obligations**"), the Claims Period shall continue indefinitely;

(b) with respect to Buyer Losses arising under (i) 0 or (a) with respect any breach or inaccuracy of any representation or warranty in 0 (Tax Returns; Taxes) (the "**Tax Representations**") or (ii) (d) (the

"**Tax Obligations**"), the Claims Period shall continue until ninety (90) days after the expiration of any applicable statute of limitations relating to the rights of any third party to bring any claim with respect to such matters;

(c) with respect to Seller Losses arising under (a), the Claims Period shall continue indefinitely, except as limited by Law (including any applicable statutes of limitation); and

(d) with respect to all other Buyer Losses or Seller Losses arising under this Agreement, the Claims Period shall terminate on the date that is twenty-four (24) months after the Closing Date.

Notwithstanding the foregoing, if, prior to the close of business on the last day of the applicable Claims Period, an Indemnifying Party shall have been properly notified of a claim for indemnity under this Agreement and such claim shall not have been finally resolved or disposed of at such date, such claim shall continue to survive and shall remain a basis for indemnity under this Agreement until such claim is finally resolved or disposed of in accordance with the terms of this Agreement.

Section 7.05 Liability Limits. The Buyer Indemnified Parties shall not make a claim for indemnification under 0 for Buyer Losses unless and until the aggregate amount of such Buyer Losses exceeds [________ Dollars ($•)] (the "**Basket**"), in which case the Buyer Indemnified Parties may claim indemnification for the full amount of such Buyer Losses; provided, however, neither the Surviving Representations nor the Tax Representations shall be subject to the Basket. The total aggregate amount of the liability of the Seller for Buyer Losses shall be limited to [________ Dollars ($•)] (the "**Cap**"); provided, however, that the Surviving Obligations, the Surviving Representations, the Tax Obligations and the Tax Representations shall not be subject to the Cap; provided, further, that the total aggregate amount of liability of the Seller for Buyer Losses arising under 0 with respect to any breach or inaccuracy of any of the Surviving Representations or Tax Representations, and the Surviving Obligations and the Tax Obligations shall be limited to an aggregate amount equal to the Purchase Price.

Section 7.06 Determination of Losses. In calculating the amount of any Buyer Losses arising from a breach of any representation, warranty or covenant contained in this Agreement which is qualified by the words "material," "in all material respects," "Material Adverse Effect" or similar terms, or by a specific dollar threshold, such Buyer Losses shall be calculated as if such qualifier or threshold were not contained therein, it being understood that the exclusion of such qualifier or threshold shall apply solely for the purpose of calculation of Buyer Losses, and not for the purpose of determining whether or not such a breach has occurred.

Section 7.07 Investigations. The respective representations and warranties of the Parties contained in this Agreement or any certificate or other document delivered by any Party at or prior to the Closing and the rights to indemnification set forth in this 0 shall not be deemed waived or otherwise affected by any investigation made, or knowledge acquired, by a Party.

Section 7.08 Treatment of Indemnification Payments. All payments made pursuant to this 0 shall be deemed adjustments to the Purchase Price for Tax purposes.

Section 7.09 Exclusive Remedies. Each Party acknowledges and agrees that, except for (a) any claim for injunctive or other equitable relief pursuant to 0 or (b) any claim related to any criminal activity, fraud or intentional misrepresentation by the other Party in connection with the Transactions, its sole and exclusive remedy with respect to any and all claims for any Legal Dispute shall be pursuant to the indemnification provisions set forth in this 0.

ARTICLE VIII
MISCELLANEOUS PROVISIONS

Section 8.01 Notices. All notices, communications, consents and deliveries under this Agreement shall be delivered in writing, unless otherwise expressly permitted herein, and shall be deemed given: (a) when delivered if delivered personally (including by courier); (b) on the third day after mailing, if mailed, postage prepaid, by registered or certified mail (return receipt requested); (c) on the day after mailing if sent by a nationally recognized overnight delivery service which maintains records of the time, place and receipt of delivery; or (d) upon receipt of a confirmed transmission, if sent by telex, telecopy or facsimile transmission, in each case to the parties at the following addresses or to such other addresses as may be furnished in writing by one Party to the others:

To the Buyer: [__________________]
[__________________]
[__________________]
Attn: [__________________]
Fax: [__________________]

with a copy to: [__________________]
[__________________]
[__________________]
Attn: [__________________]
Fax: [__________________]

and

[__________________]
[__________________]
[__________________]
Attn: [__________________]
Fax: [__________________]

To the Seller: [__________________]
[__________________]
[__________________]
Attn: [__________________]
Fax: [__________________]

with a copy to: [__________________]
[__________________]
[__________________]
Attn: [__________________]
Fax: [__________________]

Section 8.02 <u>Schedules and Exhibits</u>. The Schedules and Exhibits are hereby incorporated into this Agreement and are hereby made a part of this Agreement as if set out in full in this Agreement.

Section 8.03 <u>Assignment; Successors in Interest</u>. No assignment or transfer by any Party of such Party's rights and obligations under this Agreement shall be made except with the prior written consent of the other Party; <u>provided, however</u>, that the Buyer shall, without the obligation to obtain the prior written consent of any other Party, be entitled to assign this Agreement or all or any part of its rights or obligations under this Agreement to any of the Buyer's Affiliates, any lenders for collateral or other purposes, or to any subsequent purchaser of all or substantially all of the stock or assets of the Acquired Companies; provided that no such assignment shall release the Buyer of its obligations under this Agreement. This Agreement shall be binding upon and shall inure to the benefit of the Parties and their respective successors and permitted assigns, and any reference to a Party shall also be a reference to the successors and permitted assigns thereof.

Section 8.04 Captions. The titles, captions and table of contents contained in this Agreement are inserted in this Agreement only as a matter of convenience and for reference and in no way define, limit, extend or describe the scope of this Agreement or the intent of any provision of this Agreement.

Section 8.05 Controlling Law; Amendment. This Agreement shall be governed by and construed and enforced in accordance with the internal Laws of the State of Delaware without reference to its choice of law rules. This Agreement may not be amended, modified or supplemented except by written agreement of the Parties.

Section 8.06 Consent to Jurisdiction, Etc. Each Party hereby irrevocably agrees that any Legal Dispute shall be brought only to the exclusive jurisdiction of the courts of the State of Delaware or the federal courts located in the State of Delaware, and each Party hereby consents to the jurisdiction of such courts (and of the appropriate appellate courts therefrom) in any such suit, action or proceeding and irrevocable waives, to the fullest extent permitted by Law, any objection that it may now or hereafter have to the laying of the venue of any such suit, action or proceeding in any such court or that they any such suit, action or proceeding that is brought in any such court has been brought in an inconvenient forum. During the period a Legal Dispute that is filed in accordance with this 0 is pending before a court, all actions, suits or proceedings with respect to such Legal Dispute or any other Legal Dispute, including any counterclaim, cross-claim or interpleader, shall be subject to the exclusive jurisdiction of such court. Each Party hereby waives, and shall not assert as a defense in any Legal Dispute, that (a) such Party is not subject thereto, (b) such action, suit or proceeding may not be brought or is not maintainable in such court, (c) such Party's property is exempt or immune from execution, (d) such action, suit or proceeding is brought in an inconvenient forum, or (e) the venue of such action, suit or proceeding is improper. A final judgment in any action, suit or proceeding described in this 0 following the expiration of any period permitted for appeal and subject to any stay during appeal shall be conclusive and may be enforced in other jurisdictions by suit on the judgment or in any other manner provided by applicable Laws.

Section 8.07 Severability. Any provision of this Agreement that is prohibited or unenforceable in any jurisdiction shall, as to such jurisdiction, be ineffective to the extent of such prohibition or unenforceability without invalidating the remaining provisions of this Agreement, and any such prohibition or unenforceability in any jurisdiction shall not invalidate or render unenforceable such provision in any other jurisdiction. To the extent permitted by Law, each Party hereby waives any provision of law that renders any such provision prohibited or unenforceable in any respect.

Section 8.08 Counterpart Signature Pages; Electronic Delivery. This Agreement may be executed in multiple signature pages (including by means of telecopied or e-mailed signature pages), any one of which need not contain the signatures of more than one Party, but all such signature pages taken together shall constitute one and the same instrument. This Agreement and any signed agreement or instrument entered into in connection with this Agreement, and any amendments hereto or thereto, to the extent signed and delivered by means of a PDF email, shall be treated in all manner and respects as an original agreement or instrument and shall be considered to have the same binding legal effect as if it were the original signed version thereof delivered in person. At the request of any Party hereto or to any such agreement or instrument, each other Party hereto or thereto shall re-execute original forms thereof and deliver them to all other Parties. No Party hereto or to any such agreement or instrument shall raise the use of a PDF email to deliver a signature or the fact that any signature or agreement or instrument was transmitted or communicated through the use of a PDF email as a defense to the formation of a contract and each such Party forever waives any such defense.

Section 8.09 Enforcement of Certain Rights. Nothing expressed or implied in this Agreement is intended, or shall be construed, to confer upon or give any Person other than the Parties, and their successors or permitted assigns, any right, remedy, obligation or liability under or by reason of this Agreement, or result in such Person being deemed a third-party beneficiary of this Agreement.

Section 8.10 Waiver. Any agreement on the part of a Party to any extension or waiver of any provision of this Agreement shall be valid only if set forth in an instrument in writing signed on behalf of such Party. A waiver by a Party of the performance of any covenant, agreement, obligation, condition, representation or warranty shall not be construed as a waiver of any other covenant, agreement, obligation, condition, representation or warranty. A waiver by any Party of the performance of any act shall not constitute a waiver of the performance of any other act or an identical act required to be performed at a later time.

Section 8.11 Integration. This Agreement and the documents executed pursuant to this Agreement supersede all negotiations, agreements and understandings among the Parties with respect to the subject matter of this Agreement (except for that certain Confidentiality Agreement, dated as of **[________ ___, 20__]**, by and between [______] and [______]) and constitute the entire agreement among the Parties with respect thereto.

Section 8.12 Specific Performance. Each Party acknowledges and agrees that the non-breaching Party would suffer irreparable damage if any provision of this Agreement were not performed in accordance with its specific terms or were otherwise breached. Accordingly, each Party agrees that, in the event of any breach or threatened breach by the other Party of any covenant or obligation contained in this Agreement, (a) the non-breaching Party shall be entitled (in addition to any other remedy that may be available to it whether in law or equity, including monetary damages) to seek and obtain (i) a decree or order of specific performance to enforce the observance and performance of such covenant or obligation, and (ii) an injunction restraining such breach or threatened breach, and (b) it will not assert, and hereby does, waive, in any action for specific performance, the defense of adequacy of a remedy at law. Each Party further agrees that neither the other Party nor any other Person shall be required to obtain, furnish or post any bond or similar instrument in connection with or as a condition to obtaining any remedy referred to in this 0, and each Party irrevocably waives any right it may have to require the obtaining, furnishing or posting of any such bond or similar instrument.

Section 8.13 Transaction Costs. Except as provided above or as otherwise expressly provided in this Agreement, (a) the Buyer shall pay its own fees, costs and expenses incurred in connection herewith and the Transactions, including the fees, costs and expenses of its financial advisors, accountants and counsel, and (b) at the Closing, the Seller shall pay the fees, costs and expenses of the Seller and the Company incurred in connection herewith and the Transactions, including the fees, costs and expenses of their respective financial advisors, accountants and counsel.

ARTICLE IX
DEFINITIONS; CONSTRUCTION

Section 9.01 Definitions. The following terms, as used in this Agreement, have the following meanings:

"**Acquisition**" has the meaning given to such term in the recitals of this Agreement.

"**Action**" means any claim, suit, action, proceeding, arbitration, application, litigation, lawsuit, hearing, inquiry, complaint, charge or investigation by or before any Governmental Entity and any appeal from any of the foregoing.

"**Affiliate**" of any particular Person means any other Person controlling, controlled by or under common control with such particular Person. For the purposes of this definition, "control" means the possession, directly or indirectly, of the power to direct the management and policies of a Person whether through the ownership of voting securities, contract or otherwise.

"**Agreement**" means this Stock Purchase Agreement as the same may be amended, supplemented or otherwise modified from time to time, this "**Agreement**".

"**Applicable Benefit Laws**" means all Laws or other legislative, administrative or judicial promulgations, other than ERISA and the Code, including those of a jurisdiction outside the United State of America, applicable to any Company Benefit Plan or ERISA Affiliate Plan.

"**Audited Financial Statements**" has the meaning given to such term in (a).

"**Balance Sheet**" has the meaning given to such term in (a).

"**Basket**" has the meaning given to such term in 0.

"**Buyer**" has the meaning given to such term in the preamble of this Agreement.

"**Buyer Ancillary Document**" means any certificate, agreement, document or other instrument, other than this Agreement, to be executed and delivered by the Buyer in connection with the transactions contemplated by this Agreement.

"**Buyer Indemnified Parties**" means the Buyer and its Affiliates, each of their respective officers, directors, employees, agents and representatives and each of the heirs, executors, successors and assigns of any of the foregoing.

"**Buyer Losses**" has the meaning given to such term in 0.

"**Business**" has the meaning given to such term in the recitals of this Agreement.

"**Business Day**" means any day except Saturday, Sunday or any day on which banks are generally not open for business in New York, New York.

"**Cap**" has the meaning given to such term in 0.

"**CERCLA**" means the United States Comprehensive Environmental Response, Compensation and Liability Act and the rules and regulations promulgated thereunder.

"**Claims Period**" means the period during which a claim for indemnification may be asserted under this Agreement by an Indemnified Party.

"**Closing**" has the meaning given to such term in 0.

"**Code**" means the United States Internal Revenue Code of 1986, as amended.

"**Company**" has the meaning given to such term in the recitals of this Agreement.

"**Company Affiliated Person**" means (a) any shareholder, director or officer of the Company, (b) any individual with whom any shareholder, director or officer of the Company has any direct or indirect relation by blood, marriage or adoption (a "**Family Member**"), (c) any entity in which any shareholder, director or officer of the Company or any of his or her Family Members owns any beneficial interest (other than a publicly held corporation whose stock is traded on a national securities exchange or in the over-the-counter market and less than 5% of the stock of which is beneficially owned by all such shareholders, directors, officers and Persons in the aggregate), or (d) any Affiliate of any shareholder, director or officer of the Company or any of his or her Family Members.

"**Company Ancillary Document**" means any certificate, agreement, document or other instrument, other than this Agreement, to be executed and delivered by the Company in connection with the Transactions.

"**Company Benefit Plan**" means each Employee Benefit Plan sponsored or maintained or required to be sponsored or maintained at any time by the Company or to which the Company makes or has made, or has or has had an obligation to make, contributions at any time or with respect to which the Company has any liability, whether direct or indirect or contingent or otherwise.

"**Company Intellectual Property**" means any Intellectual Property that is owned by or licensed to the Company, including the Company Software.

"**Company Leased Real Property**" has the meaning given to such term in (a).

"**Company Licensed Software**" means all software (other than Company Proprietary Software) used by the Company.

"**Company Owned Real Property**" has the meaning given to such term in 0.

"**Company Proprietary Software**" means all software owned by the Company.

"**Company Real Property**" has the meaning given to such term in (a).

"**Company Registered Intellectual Property**" means all of the Registered Intellectual Property owned by, filed in the name of, or licensed to the Company.

"**Company Shares**" has the meaning given to such term in the recitals of this Agreement.

"**Company Software**" means the Company Licensed Software and the Company Proprietary Software.

"**Confidential Information**" means all non-public and all proprietary information relating to the Company or the Business, including, the terms of this Agreement and any related transactions.

"**Contract**" means any agreement, contract, commitment, lease, license, arrangement, consensual obligation, understanding, promise or undertaking, (whether written or oral and whether express or implied), whether or not legally binding.

"**Customers**" means each Person that is a customer of the Company as of the date of this Agreement that paid the Company in the aggregate more than $[•] during the twelve (12)-month period ended [________ __, 20__].

"**Disclosure Schedules**" has the meaning given to such term in (f).

"**Employee Benefit Plan**" means, with respect to any Person, (a) each plan, fund, program, agreement, arrangement or scheme, including each plan, fund, program, agreement, arrangement or scheme maintained or required to be maintained under the Laws of a jurisdiction outside the United States of America, in each case, that is at any time sponsored or maintained or required to be sponsored or maintained by such Person or to which such Person makes or has made, or has or has had any liability, whether direct or indirect or contingent or otherwise, with respect to, or any obligation to make, contributions providing for employee benefits or for the remuneration, direct or indirect, of the employees, former employees, directors, managers, officers, consultants, independent contractors, contingent workers or leased employees of such Person or the dependents of any of them (whether written or oral), including each deferred compensation, bonus, incentive compensation, pension, retirement, stock purchase, stock option and other equity compensation plan, "welfare" plan (within the meaning of Section 3(1) of ERISA, determined without regard to whether such plan is subject to ERISA), (b) each "pension" plan (within the meaning of Section 3(2) of ERISA, determined without regard to whether such plan is subject to ERISA), (c) each employment, change of control, severance plan or agreement, health, vacation, summer hours, supplemental unemployment benefit, hospitalization insurance, medical, dental, legal, and (d) each other employee benefit plan, fund, program, agreement, arrangement or scheme.

"**Employment Agreement**" means any employment Contract, consulting agreement, termination or severance agreement, change of control agreement or any other agreement respecting the terms and conditions of employment or payment of compensation, or of a consulting or independent contractor relationship in respect to any current or former officer, employee, consultant or independent contractor.

"**Environmental Laws**" means all local, state and federal Laws relating to protection of surface or ground water, drinking water supply, soil, surface or subsurface strata or medium, or ambient air, pollution control, product registration and Hazardous Materials.

"**ERISA**" means the United States Employee Retirement Income Security Act of 1974 and the rules and regulations promulgated thereunder.

"**ERISA Affiliate**" means any Person (whether incorporated or unincorporated) that together with any Acquired Company would be deemed a "single employer" within the meaning of Section 414 of the Code.

"**ERISA Affiliate Plan**" means each Employee Benefit Plan sponsored or maintained or required to be sponsored or maintained at any time by any ERISA Affiliate, or to which such ERISA Affiliate makes or has made, or has or has had an obligation to make, contributions at any time or with respect to which any ERISA Affiliate has any liability, whether direct or indirect or contingent or otherwise.

"**Financial Statements**" has the meaning given to such term in (a).

"**FLSA**" means the United States Fair Labor Standards Act and the rules and regulations promulgated thereunder.

"**GAAP**" means generally accepted accounting principles as applied in the United States.

"**Governmental Entity**" means any federal, state or local or foreign government, any political subdivision thereof or any court, administrative or regulatory agency, department, instrumentality, body or commission or other governmental authority or agency, domestic or foreign.

"**Hazardous Materials**" means any waste, pollutant, contaminant, hazardous substance, toxic, ignitable, reactive or corrosive substance, hazardous waste, special waste, industrial substance, by-product, process-intermediate product or waste, petroleum or petroleum-derived substance or waste, chemical liquids or solids, liquid or gaseous products, or any constituent of any such substance or waste, the use, handling or disposal of which by the Company is in any way governed by or subject to any applicable Law.

"**Indemnified Party**" has the meaning given to such term in 0.

"**Indemnifying Party**" has the meaning given to such term in 0.

"**Insurance Policy**" has the meaning given to such term in 0.

"**Intellectual Property**" means all intellectual property and other similar proprietary rights in any jurisdiction throughout the world, whether owned or held for use under license, whether registered or unregistered, including such rights in and to: (a) trademarks, trade dress, service marks, certification marks, logos, trade names, corporate names, assumed names and brand names and other indications of origin (collectively, "**Trademarks**"); (b) patents and patent applications, and any and all divisions, continuations, continuations-in-part, reissues, continuing patent applications, reexaminations, and extensions thereof, any counterparts claiming priority therefrom, utility models, certificates of invention, certificates of registration and like rights (collectively, "**Patents**"); inventions, invention disclosures, discoveries and improvements, whether or not patentable; (c) writings and other works of authorship, copyright registrations, copyright applications and unregistered common law copyrights, author's rights and photographic releases; (d) trade secrets (including those trade secrets defined in the Uniform Trade Secrets Act and under corresponding foreign Law and common law) and other confidential or non-public business information, including ideas, formulas, compositions, inventions, discoveries and improvements, know-how, manufacturing and production processes and techniques, research and development information, drawings, specifications, designs, plans, proposals, technical data, financial, marketing and business data, pricing and cost information, business and marketing plans and customer and supplier lists and information, in each case whether or not patentable or copyrightable, and rights to limit the use or disclosure thereof by any Person (collectively, "**Trade Secrets**"); (e) computer software, including programs, source code, object code, algorithms, application programming interfaces, databases and other software-related specifications and documentation (collectively, "**Software**"); (f) all internet protocol addresses and networks, including domain names, internet e-mail addresses, world wide web (www) and http addresses, network names, network addresses and services (such as mail or website) whether or not used or currently in service and any registrations relating thereto; (g) moral rights and design rights; (h) the goodwill associated with each of the foregoing; (i) all licenses for Intellectual Property for any of the above listed items; and (j) claims, causes of action and defenses relating to the enforcement of any of the foregoing; in each case, including any registrations of, applications to register, and renewals and extensions of, any of the foregoing with or by any Governmental Entity in any jurisdiction. Intellectual Property includes all copies and tangible embodiments of the foregoing (in whatever medium), and any other similar intellectual property rights actually used in connection with the business activities and endeavors of the Company.

"**Knowledge**" with respect to the Seller means (a) all facts known by each of the directors and officers of the Company after due inquiry and diligence with respect to the matters at hand, and (b) all facts that any of the foregoing individuals should have known with respect to the matters at hand if such individual had made due inquiry and exercised reasonable diligence.

"**Labor Laws**" means all Laws and all contracts or collective bargaining agreements governing or concerning labor relations, unions and collective bargaining, terms and conditions of employment, employment discrimination, harassment, and retaliation, wages, hours or occupational safety and health, including, the United States Immigration Reform and Control Act of 1986, the United States National Labor Relations Act, the United States Civil Rights Acts of 1866 and 1964, the United States Equal Pay Act, WARN, ERISA, the United States Family and Medical Leave Act, the United States Americans with Disabilities Act, the United States Age Discrimination in Employment Act, the United States Davis Bacon Act, the

United States Walsh-Healy Act, the United States Service Contract Act, United States Executive Order 11246, FLSA and the United States Rehabilitation Act of 1973, any state, local or foreign counterparts, and all rules and regulations promulgated under such acts.

"**Laws**" means all statutes, rules, codes, regulations, restrictions, ordinances, orders, decrees, approvals, directives, judgments, injunctions, writs, awards and decrees of, or issued by, all Governmental Entities.

"**Legal Dispute**" means any action, suit or proceeding between or among the Parties and their respective Affiliates arising in connection with any disagreement, dispute, controversy or claim arising out of or relating to this Agreement or any related document.

"**Liabilities**" or "**Liability**" means debts, liabilities, commitments and obligations (including guarantees and other forms of credit support), whether accrued or fixed, absolute or contingent, matured or unmatured, on- or off-balance sheet, including those arising under any Law or Action and those arising under any Contract or otherwise.

"**Licenses**" means all notifications, licenses, permits (including environmental, construction and operation permits), franchises, certificates, approvals, exemptions, classifications, registrations and other similar documents and authorizations issued by any Governmental Entity, and applications therefor.

"**Liens**" mean all mortgages, liens, pledges, security interests, charges, claims, restrictions and encumbrances of any nature whatsoever.

"**Loss**" means any claim, liability, obligation, loss, cost, Tax, expense, penalty, fine or judgment (at equity or at law, including statutory and common) and damage whenever arising or incurred (including amounts paid in settlement, costs of investigation and reasonable attorneys' fees and expenses).

"**Material Adverse Effect**" means any state of facts, change, event, effect or occurrence that shall have occurred or been threatened (when taken together with all other states of fact, changes, events, effects or occurrences that have occurred or been threatened) that is or could be reasonably likely to be materially adverse to the financial condition, results of operations, properties, assets or liabilities (including contingent liabilities) of the Company, or the real or personal property of the Company, taken as a whole. A Material Adverse Effect shall also include any state of facts, change, event or occurrence that shall have occurred or been threatened (when taken together with all other states of facts, changes, events, effects or occurrences that have occurred or been threatened) that is or could be reasonably likely to prevent or materially delay the performance by the Company of its obligations under this Agreement or the consummation of any of the Transactions.

"**Material Contract**" and "**Material Contracts**" have the meanings given to such terms in 0.

"**NLRB**" means the United States National Labor Relations Board.

"**Order**" means any order, award, injunction, judgment, decree, ruling, directive, determination, subpoena or verdict or other decision issued by a Governmental Entity.

"**Ordinary Course**" means, with respect to the Company, the ordinary course of the Company's business consistent with its past practices.

"**Organizational Documents**" means (a) the certificate of incorporation; (b) articles of incorporation; (c) articles of organization; (d) bylaws; (e) any charter or similar document adopted or filed in connection with the creation, formation or organization of a Person; and (f) any amendment to any of the foregoing.

"**Permits**" has the meaning given to such term in (a).

"**Permitted Liens**" means (a) Liens for Taxes not yet due and payable, (b) statutory Liens of landlords, (c) Liens of carriers, warehousemen, mechanics, materialmen and repairmen incurred in the Ordinary Course and not yet delinquent, and (d) in the case of Real Property, zoning, building, or other restrictions, variances, covenants, rights of way, encumbrances, easements and other minor irregularities in title, none of which, individually or in the aggregate, (i) interfere in any material respect with the present use of or occupancy of the affected parcel by the Company, (ii) have more than an immaterial effect on the value thereof or its use, or (iii) would impair the ability of such parcel to be sold for its present use.

"**Person**" means any individual, corporation, partnership, joint venture, limited liability company, trust, unincorporated organization or Governmental Entity.

"**Purchase Price**" has the meaning given to such term in 0.

"**Receivables**" has the meaning given to such term in (a).

"**Registered Intellectual Property**" means all United States, international and foreign: (a) Patents; (b) Trademarks; (c) registered copyrights and applications for copyright registration; (d) domain name registrations; and (e) any other Intellectual Property that is the subject of an application, certificate, filing, registration or other document issued, filed with, or recorded with any federal, state, local or foreign Governmental Entity or other public body.

"**Release**" means, with respect to any Hazardous Material, any spilling, leaking, pumping, pouring, emitting, emptying, discharging, injecting, escaping, leaching, dumping or disposing into any surface or ground water, drinking water supply, soil, surface or subsurface strata or medium, or the ambient air.

"**Representative**" means, with respect to any Person, any director, officer, manager, partner, member, equity holder, agent, employee, attorney, broker, lender, financing source, advisor or other representative of such Person.

"**Schedule**" has the meaning given to such term in (f).

"**Seller Ancillary Document**" means any certificate, agreement, document or other instrument, other than this Agreement, to be executed and delivered by a Seller in connection with the Transactions.

"**Seller Indemnified Parties**" means the Sellers, and their respective heirs, executors, successors and assigns of any of the foregoing.

"**Seller Losses**" has the meaning given to such term in Section 10.02.

"**Suppliers**" means any supplier that the Acquired Companies have paid in the aggregate more than $[•] during the twelve (12)-month period ended [________ __, 20__].

“**Surviving Obligations**” has the meaning given to such term in (a).

“**Surviving Representations**” has the meaning given to such term in (a).

“**Taxes**” means all taxes, assessments, charges, duties, fees, levies and other governmental charges, including income, franchise, capital stock, real property, personal property, tangible, withholding, employment, payroll, social security, social contribution, unemployment compensation, disability, transfer, sales, use, excise, gross receipts, escheat, value-added and all other taxes of any kind for which the Company may have any liability imposed by any Governmental Entity, whether disputed or not, and any charges, interest or penalties imposed by any Governmental Entity.

“**Tax Obligations**” has the meaning given to such term in (a).

“**Tax Representations**” has the meaning given to such term in (a).

“**Tax Return**” means any report, return, declaration or other information required to be supplied to a Governmental Entity in connection with Taxes, including estimated and amended returns.

“**Transactions**” has the meaning given to such term in the recitals to this Agreement.

“**Treasury Regulations**” means the Income Tax Regulations promulgated under the Code.

“**Unaudited Financial Statements**” has the meaning given to such term in (a).

“**WARN**” means the United States Worker Adjustment and Retraining Notification Act and the rules and regulations promulgated thereunder.

Section 9.02 Construction.

(a) Unless otherwise set forth in this Agreement, all references to Articles, Sections, subsections, Schedules and Exhibits are to Articles, Sections, subsections, Schedules and Exhibits in or to this Agreement.

(b) Unless the context of this Agreement explicitly requires otherwise, (i) references to the plural include the singular, and references to the singular include the plural, (ii) references to any gender include the other genders, (iii) the words "hereof," "herein" and "hereunder" and words of similar import refer to this Agreement as a whole and not to any particular provision of this Agreement, (iv) the words "include," "includes,' and "including" are not limiting and shall be deemed to be followed by the words "without limitation", (v) the terms "day" and "days" mean and refer to calendar days, (vi) the terms "year" and "years" mean and refer to calendar years, and (vii) all references to "dollars" or "$" means the lawful currency of the United States of America and the settlement of all payments under this Agreement shall be made in such currency.

(c) All accounting terms not specifically defined herein shall be construed in accordance with GAAP.

(d) In the computation of periods of time from a specified date to a later specified date, the word "from" means "from and including"; the words "to" and "until" each mean "to but excluding"; and the word "through" means "to and including."

(e) The Article and Section headings herein are for convenience only and shall not affect the construction hereof.

(f) This Agreement is the result of negotiations among and has been reviewed by each Party's counsel. Accordingly, this Agreement shall not be construed against any Party merely because of such Party's involvement in its preparation.

(g) The disclosure schedules delivered by the Seller to the Buyer immediately prior to the Parties' execution and delivery of this Agreement (each, a "**Schedule**," and collectively, the "**Disclosure Schedules**"), are arranged for convenience of reference in Schedules corresponding to the numbered and lettered Sections in this Agreement. Disclosure of any fact or item in any Schedule shall qualify the corresponding Section of this Agreement and shall be deemed to have been disclosed with respect to every other Section of this Agreement only to the extent that such Schedule is cross-referenced in any other Schedule. Capitalized terms used in the Disclosure Schedules and not otherwise defined therein have the meanings given to such terms in this Agreement.

(h) Unless otherwise set forth in this Agreement, references in this Agreement to (i) any document, instrument, contract or agreement (including this Agreement) (A) includes and incorporates all exhibits, schedules and other attachments thereto, (B) includes all documents, instruments, contracts or agreements issued or executed in replacement thereof, and (C) means such document, instrument, contracts or agreement, or replacement or predecessor thereto, as amended, restated, supplemented or otherwise modified from time to time in accordance with its terms and in effect at any given time, and (ii) a particular Law means such Law as amended, modified, supplemented or succeeded, from time to time and in effect at any given time.

[Signature Page Follows]

IN WITNESS WHEREOF, the Parties have caused this Agreement to be duly executed, as of the date first above written.

THE BUYER:

[________________]

By: ______________________________
Name:
Title:

THE SELLER:

[________________]

By: ______________________________
Name:
Title:

ABOUT THE AUTHORS

Jaron R. Brown is Director, Assistant General Counsel for Novelis Inc. At Novelis, Mr. Brown is the corporate legal office's lead attorney for managing negotiation, drafting, and counseling with respect to all contracts of the commercial department and the global procurement department. He also has responsibilities related to securities, M&A, finance, and compliance. Prior to joining Novelis, Mr. Brown was a partner with the law firm of King & Spalding and a member of the firm's Corporate Practice Group. While at King & Spalding, Mr. Brown represented private equity funds and public and private companies in strategic transactions, such as mergers, acquisitions, divestitures, and capital raising transactions. Mr. Brown is a graduate of Case Western Reserve University School of Law, and a graduate of the University of Hartford in West Hartford, Connecticut, where he was a scholarship member of the men's Division I basketball team. On a personal note, Mr. Brown is a husband and a father of two, with a third on the way.

Tyler E. Giles is currently a Partner in the Corporate Group of FisherBroyles LLP. Prior to joining FisherBroyles, Mr. Giles served as Senior Director and Corporate Counsel for Equifax Inc., where he advised the corporate development team on mergers and acquisitions and the emerging markets team in general corporate matters. Mr. Giles has counseled clients in connection with transactions touching six of the seven continents and has extensive experience closing M&A deals in Central and South America. Mr. Giles received his Juris Doctorate degree, magna cum laude, from the University of Georgia School of Law, and was inducted into the Order of the Coif upon graduation. He received his Bachelor's in Business Administration, Magna Cum Laude, from Georgia State University, where he was awarded the Dean's Key, the Faculty Scholarship Award and the Francis R. Bridges Scholastic Achievement Award. Mr. Giles can be reached at giles@tylergiles.com.

ASPATORE